FROM
GRENADES
TO
GRIDDLES
AND EVERYTHING
IN BETWEEN

A HISTORY OF
CHAMBERLIN AND HILL

NATASHA WILSON

First published in 2023 by
Free Association Books

Copyright © 2023 Chamberlin and Hill

The author's rights are fully asserted. The right of
Natasha Wilson to be identified as the author of this work
has been asserted by her in accordance with the
Copyright, Designs and Patents Act 1988

A CIP Catalogue of this book is available from
the British Library

ISBN: 978-19113838-5-7

Cover design and typeset by
www.chandlerbookdesign.com

Printed in Great Britain by
Short Run Press Ltd.

CONTENTS

1

Walsall, United Kingdom,
present day …

f you travel through Middle Earth – sorry, the West Midlands – you might find yourself in Walsall, a small town to the northwest of Birmingham. But if you, like me, have a habit of bringing home a fridge magnet from any place you visit, forget it. Walsall's High Street doesn't have an Information Centre with colourful displays offering maps of the area, leaflets about the sites of interest, mugs covered in prints of local "beauty spots" and various other bits of heart-warming kitsch. I suppose this is because Walsall, unlike many English towns and cities, doesn't consider itself to be glamorous enough for such self advertising. It can't lure you in by the promise of a magnificent cathedral, a giant armadillo-like shopping arcade or romantic ruins of a mediaeval castle. Walsall is about something different. It is an industrial hub. Its "places of interest" are not splendid, picturesque or alluring – but, without them, all of the UK's eye-pleasing tourist Meccas, guidebooks' favourites, would struggle to exist and function the way they do. Today I am going to one of these places. Follow me if you dare...

The moment you walk through this building's door, every one of your senses will get a mighty punch. The smell, overwhelming, "with a hint of salty smoke", but not really matching any of the odours your nose has ever been exposed to before, will seep into your hair and your clothes and secretly linger there for a while. It's a peculiar smell: more alien than unpleasant, more warning than threatening, it nevertheless sends a ridiculous thought tumbling through your mind: could this have been what those folks from Pompeii had sniffed in the air a day or two before good old Vesuvius showed the world his true nature?

And there is noise. Then again, this is not quite the right word for what you'll hear. Neighbours partying next door make noise. The sound that will hit your eardrums in this place is a deep, low-pitched, painfully vibrating growling of a thousand dragons, punctuated by heavy but strangely sonorous drumming, and garnished with screechy cries of invisible prehistoric monsters. This audio cocktail is evenly dispersed in the space around; it penetrates and saturates every grain of this space, becoming part of it. You will hear it, loud and clear, through the soft squashy plugs you have stuck into your ears: without them, you won't last here long enough to see what we came here to see…

So let's go and take a look. We will move through the enormous, hangar-sized room, filled with grey, all fifty shades of it: taupe floor, darkened in places by shallow puddles; light pewter walls; pipes and rods of various metallic hues seemingly chaotically stretched underneath a very high caliginous ceiling. But there are other colours too. We will carefully manoeuvre between rows of tall racks: some green, some blue, all stuffed with heavy boxes. We'll have to watch out for fast-moving black-and-orange forklifts that suddenly appear from around the corner, carrying their softly glistening cargo about this weird and wonderful world. And, just when we think that we've learnt to cope with all the unusualness surrounding us and are beginning to relax, comes another punch. This one is a knockout.

Some twenty yards ahead of us is a firefall. That's right, like in "a waterfall", only here, instead of water, a stream of furious flames pours down from somewhere above. We don't need to step any closer to feel the heat, its degree betrayed by the colour. The flames, blindingly, wrathfully white and adorned with ragged yellow fringes, are far hotter than the timid orangey red of the annual bonfire at the back of your garden. The floor in front of them is covered in uneven grey waves: the heat has melted the concrete. Hundreds of sparks are frantically dancing around like huge rabid wasps. God forbid you come near enough for one of them to sting you; these flying beasts are, in fact, droplets of insanely hot fluid metal. The stream of flames, the firefall, is molten iron: something that we, mere mortals, are not meant to be able to witness, as the only place on Earth where iron can be found in its liquid form is nearly 2000 miles beneath our feet, in the very core of the planet. Luckily, having discovered how useful this metal can be, humankind has managed to find a loophole in nature's unwritten Code of Laws. And that is precisely where we are now: in this loophole, aka a foundry. Tucked in between neat rows of ordinary houses and lines of cars parked along the streets of Walsall, this site with several architecturally unpretentious buildings is a part of Chamberlin and Hill Castings, a company whose name might not be coming up in a pub quiz or lurking in the list of the main attractions of Great Britain. Yet our daily life depends heavily on its foundries' gates being open and its furnaces spitting out fluid fire: a bit cooler than the Sun, a bit hotter than an erupting volcano...

2

… and 130 years earlier

That evening The Woodman was even fuller than could be expected on an indolent Saturday night of July. Was it just one of those inexplicable surprises that life often bestows upon people without their consent or was it an inevitable consequence of a profoundly disturbing invasion of Boreas, with his wintry manner, onto the territory of the temperamental British summer in 1888? One way or the other, the crowd of red-faced men, each of them clad in dark loose-fitting trouser-and-jacket set and displaying a seemingly compulsory off-grey cap pulled low over the forehead and often boldly tilted to one side, was gathered in the pub on the border between the borough of Aston Manor and Birmingham for their well-earned end-of-the-week session of cheerful hobnobbing. The venue that evidently had seen far better days nevertheless attracted, without fail, a great number of patrons, mainly due to being strategically placed in the midst of an area densely packed with small manufacturing plants and within yards of Birmingham railway station. Visitors nursed pints of luminous amber-coloured ale in their large hands, dark from dust and grease permanently embedded into the skin, and talked in raised voices about Aston Villa joining the newly formed football league and about the freak snowfall that had suddenly descended on Birmingham last Wednesday, disturbing the habitual order of things. An occasional tirade prophesying a disastrous weather change dooming the world was immediately drowned in the waves of overall light-hearted cheerfulness.

Two gentlemen sitting at a small table in the corner of the back room, by the window facing the busy Canal Street, looked distinctly different from the rest of the crowd. Well groomed, immaculately dressed in tailored sack suits with sharp wingtip collars over four-in-hand ties, they seemed oblivious to the hubbub saturating the space around them.

The younger of the two was James William, eldest son of John and Elizabeth Chamberlin. Born in 1852 in Reading, at the moment of the conversation he was only in his mid-thirties but that didn't stop him from experiencing some sort of a mid-life crisis. It would have been perfectly natural for him to follow in the footsteps of his father, a skilful and successful hatter with his own business and enviable income, sufficient for maintaining a family with six children. But James wasn't convinced. In 1871, he got a job in a drapers' shop in Cheltenham and in a few years, having earned a reputation of a suave, reliable and hardworking salesman, moved to a prestigious **Chipperfield and Butler's** store in Brighton. It was a magnificent drapery shop offering the finest clothes, hats and linen to the town gentry. This looked like an almost perfect arrangement: the wages were decent, the employees were provided with lodgings in nearby Castle Street, and the young Chamberlin's diligence guaranteed him a steady career in retail business. Yet James had no intention of spending the rest of his life measuring trouser lengths and matching neckties to jackets of the shop's wealthy customers. He knew that his keen eye for detail and his outstanding problem solving ability (qualities that marked him as a good salesman) could be put to better use in a different setting. Besides, a young lady by the name of Edith Emma Pearton, soon to become his fiancée, had been waiting for him back in Reading, and James was determined to improve and secure his financial situation before proposing.

His companion, Henry Hill, looked a few years older. Born in 1845, he also was the eldest son in the family. But the similarity with James Chamberlin ended there. His father Stephen owned a small foundry in Foleshill, a suburb in the north of Coventry. Keen to fulfil parental expectations, Henry, together with one of his brothers, Stephen Thomas, started working at his father's plant as an iron founder. However, he seemed to be a natural at diagnosing and fixing almost every fault that frequently befell the factory's machinery, so he trained to become a mechanical engineer. Years of experience mixed with a bit of luck and a lot of elbow grease have made him a really good one. He has been content with his life. But contentment didn't fully equate to happiness: a fact of which he was acutely aware by the time he met James Chamberlin. There was also a more prosaic reason for him to be dissatisfied with his occupation: at the age of forty-three, a married man and a father of three young daughters, Henry Hill was in need of a better income.

And so it appeared that two gentlemen sitting at a small table in the corner of the back room by the window facing the busy Canal Street, despite the differences in their ages, backgrounds, occupations and experiences, had something in common: they shared ambitions, aspirations and attitude. Oh, and some ale, of course.

Talking of which, judging by the number of empty tumblers in front of them, quite a few pints had been consumed, and the conversation was rapidly approaching its finale.

— *As I was saying,* — straining his voice, continued Chamberlin who had been forced to pause mid-sentence by a particularly loud outburst of laughter from a group at the neighbouring table - *it's not so much the lack of means as the total lack of expertise that bothers me. I feel that without it I would be shooting into the brown, but investing into fine apparel is not the way forward. Not for me in any case. I wish I were…*

— *What if you had,* - interrupted Hill - *all the expertise you need and then some? With my father's imminent retirement I have been considering my own prospects and have come to the same conclusion as you…*

— *Hang on, assuming I understand correctly… are you suggesting some sort of a partnership?*

— *Well, if we go alphabetically… Here: Chamberlin and Hill! It has a certain ring to it, doesn't it?*

— *I believe it does… In this case I have a counter suggestion: why don't we take this exchange elsewhere? The din is making my head pound.*

— *Wait until you set your foot inside a foundry!* - laughed Henry, getting up and gesturing to his companion to follow him. Uttering *"Mind the grease"*, they pushed through the crowd towards the exit.

And this is how it all started.
Or is it?

3

Birmingham, United Kingdom, present day …

The unexpectedly bright April sun peeks through the window, illuminating three masked men walking slowly across an empty room. To be precise, across a tea room. It's situated in one of Birmingham's parks and is so small that, due to "social distancing", only three people at the same time are allowed there, so my companion and I have to wait our turn outside. This afternoon, just days after a slight relaxation of what seems to have been an endless lockdown, I am about to have a cappuccino (first time in over a year) – and a chat with a real foundry man (first time in my life).

Meet Gordon Stanley: a man in his early seventies, over fifty of which he has spent working for Chamberlin and Hill, rising in rank from an apprentice patternmaker to sales and commercial manager of the Bloxwich foundry. Being an employee of a business for almost half the lifetime of that business, and coming from a dynasty of men who, collectively, contributed nearly 300 years of working for the company, would automatically make him a perfect provider of memoirs which I desperately need for reconstructing the history of C&H, but this is not the reason I am talking to Gordon today. Well, not the main one. In this story my interlocutor will be wearing many hats, including the safety helmet of... well, of a foundry worker – however, right now he has a deerstalker on. For the past several weeks he has been trying to solve the mystery of the meeting of two Victorian gentlemen, the meeting that resulted in the creation of a business which took off with the speed and power of a rocket. Why was it, still is, and probably will continue to be, a mystery? As Gordon has found out, not a shred of information is left about how James William Chamberlin, a drapery salesman from East Sussex, came to know Henry Hill, a mechanical engineer based in Warwickshire, in order to establish a foundry in the West Midlands. And why on Earth would a gentleman accustomed to dealing with soft materials and refined middle class clients, an expert on sales, suddenly switch to supervising the production process in the toughest of all industries, while someone who had spent his working life stuck up to his elbows in the guts of factory machinery, fixing whatever needed to be fixed, an expert on all things heavy and metal, would abandon the manufacturing operations and turn, essentially, into a salesman? Why would they swap roles, having embarked on the most adventurous (and risky) enterprise of their lives?

Having neglected the sacred post-retirement duty of digging up his allotment, Gordon embarked on a different kind of digging. He meticulously searched the British Newspaper Archives, scanning through thousands of pages in the hope of coming across articles about the company's founders; read the documents held at Midland Bank in order to uncover records related to the purchase of land for the foundries-to-be; visited the local history archives; studied the individual family trees of both James Chamberlin and Henry Hill; obtained addresses of their namesakes on ancestry.com and wrote letters enquiring about their relatives, but received only one reply, and it wasn't helpful. The mystery fought back, refusing to be unravelled, hiding behind the wall of information deficit. And yet, slowly and hesitantly, a line and a photo at a time, the possible scenario or, rather, scenarios, of the meeting began to emerge...

We are sitting on a wooden bench outside the tearoom, holding our drinks and piles of printouts from various sites that Gordon has brought with him to show me the results of his research. My head is spinning from the abundance of names, dates and relations. They sure had big families in those days! And it seems that these family connections hold the key to the solution of the mystery. As the result of Gordon's detective work, the infinite number of ways that could have led to the meeting of Mr Chamberlin and Mr Hill was reduced to just three.

So let me start again.

4

… and 130 years earlier (take two)

I n 1875, Clara Chamberlin, James William's sister, married a gentleman called Thomas Ibbotson. The new couple opened a linen and drapers store in Hampton Street of Birmingham and were successful enough to expand the business. Soon they had another shop in town. At that time James was working in Brighton. His experience as a salesman in one of the most prestigious establishments of the seaside resort town, combined with the trustworthiness afforded a family member, would have rendered him a perfect candidate for the position of manager in one of his sister's stores. Was he invited? If so, James Chamberlin would have relocated to Warwickshire where Henry Hill was employed as a mechanical engineer at his father's foundry, and the chances of a chance meeting of the two (pun intended) would have increased dramatically. Victorian towns, including Birmingham, fast expanding and soon-to-become-a-city, offered plenty of opportunities for socialising. Does it seem a little too far-fetched? Gordon has discovered another pathway that might have led to the meeting of the future business partners: here we seem to be getting a bit warmer. This time another sibling of James's, his brother Arthur, might have served as a "missing link".

Arthur John Chamberlin… I wouldn't be able to squeeze into a whole chapter, let alone into one paragraph, all that there is to say about him. But let me try. Eight years younger than James, he started working in 1881 as an ironmonger's assistant at St Pancras in London, and only four years later, gifted with an entrepreneurship gene running in the family as well as with great communication and persuasion skills, Arthur decided to radically change his career and the direction of his life: he became a commercial traveller. He must have been exceptionally good at this job as it took him around the world; eventually he settled down in Australia where he got married and even became a local celebrity after he had helped to bring to safety Wairarapa, a ship aboard which he was travelling to New Zealand when it got damaged. Arthur and a cabin boy jumped into the heavy sea, carrying a long rope; they managed to get to the shore where the rope was fastened – as a result, 135 lives were saved! But this would happen a bit later. Now let's go back to the time when he was only establishing his reputation as a talented and somewhat lucky sales representative (this is what his job title would be today). From the few available sources we know that, amongst other companies, Arthur Chamberlin worked for **Thomas Sanders & Co** and **Wintmins & Co**, both situated in Birmingham and therefore geographically not that far from the Windmill Lane foundry in Foleshill. It's very easy to imagine the entrepreneurial and hardworking Arthur, who would have always been on the lookout for new clients, offering his services to the Hill family. Could he have knocked at that door and later befriended Henry, introducing him to his brother James who must have been getting bored of dealing with ties, hats and yards of fine cloth? This hypothetical version of events is my personal favourite, but I agree with Gordon that the most plausible one of all is what I am about to describe next…

And again, it all starts with one of James's siblings. In 1872, his sister Fanny married a master japanner, William Payne, and moved to Aston in Birmingham where her husband owned a business employing, according to the 1881 census, "4 men, 6 women and a boy". Japanning, a heavy black lacquer, was widely used by foundries for coating various home fittings, from door knockers to curtain tieback hooks. It prevented the metal from rusting and looked attractive, resembling glossy enamel paint. Not all foundries were equipped to carry on the process on their premises and some had to outsource the job to specialists like William Payne. Among those foundries looking to outsource this work could have been, and very likely was, the Windmill foundry in Foleshill. In this way, the Hill and Chamberlin families would have come across each other.

Before 1891 Fanny's husband sold his business and continued to work there as japanning foreman; another ten years later he became an

Iron founders' traveller. We have reasons to believe that it was Henry Hill who bought the factory. Studying the accounts of C&H, Gordon discovered that in December 1892 stock worth over £430 (£55,871 in today's value) was held off site in Birmingham. It's difficult to imagine that a new company would have taken this sort of risk, unless… well, unless there was no risk involved. Jumping a little ahead (spoiler alert!): when in 1903 the partnership between James Chamberlin and Henry Hill was dissolved, the latter bought his partner's half of the very same japanning factory and became its sole owner. Which means, until then, the japanning business in Aston had been an asset of C&H. Joining all the dots, we arrive at the chain of events that we believe to have led to the creation of one of the most successful and long-living iron foundries in the United Kingdom: Chuckery in Walsall.

In the mid-1880s William Payne, owner of a small but efficient japanning factory in Aston, husband of Fanny Chamberlin and by now father of four daughters and two sons, found himself in need of raising some capital. Selling his business looked like the optimal solution. At the same time, Henry Hill, working for his father, Stephen Hill, the proprietor of a small foundry in the nearby town of Foleshill and a regular customer of "Payne's Japanning works", was ready and eager to start his own enterprise. With personal savings and some help from his reasonably well-off family, Henry purchased the business. As part of the deal, William Payne continued working there as a japanning foreman, and Henry Hill, knowing that the production process was in the safe hands of the factory's ex-owner, could now concentrate on implementing his plan, which stretched far beyond continuing along the well-trodden path of the established and solvent but not excitingly prosperous business. In the months of negotiations before the sale, the budding entrepreneur had got to know a few members of William's extended family; among them was James Chamberlin, who shared his new friend's aspirations.

There is nothing surprising in the fact that two very different gentlemen with unrelated backgrounds and professions, introduced to each other through family dynamics, had similar ambitions and got on like a house on fire. Both were "children of their time", and the late Victorian Britain was not what it had been a generation prior. The rapidly emerging middle class valued perseverance above privilege, self-reliance above inherited assets. It was becoming increasingly possible and respectable to gain social and financial capital through inventiveness and enterprise, so the idea of creating a business was floating in the air along with the coal smog. Great Britain had recently entered the second stage of the Industrial Revolution, and scientific discoveries were being made at a dizzying speed, dragging the magic from fairy tales into reality. Going to the dentist was no longer an equivalent of a voluntary visit to the Holy Inquisition's torture chamber: anaesthesia started to be widely used in treatments. To move between places one no longer had to rely on equestrian skills: Karl Benz had just invented the first automobile powered by an internal combustion engine, and, to the delight of the great-great-grandpas of today's Hell's Angels, Gottlieb Daimler had introduced the first gas-engine motorcycle. Railways had become commonplace. All these, and many other innovations, were hungry consumers of energy and materials, particularly metal. The ancient craft of smelting iron was flourishing, but the rather primitive foundries which had not improved much throughout millennia needed modernisation. All that was required for creating a successful business would have been capital, expertise and zeal. Both James and Henry had bucketfuls of the latter. And, while each of them would have struggled to find enough of the former, by combining their resources and becoming partners they would have easily solved the problem. James Chamberlin would have thrown into the shared pot a sizable sum of money and his prowess in sales; Henry Hill would have added to it his engineering skills, an insider's knowledge of a foundry, as well as the japanning factory that he had bought from his brother-in-law. With or without a meaningful (and totally fictional) conversation in a cosy (and totally real) pub that I have somewhat frivolously included earlier, both partners were ready to go.

And I can say again, this time with a lot more certainty:

This is how it all started.

The rest is history.

Bloxwich Foundry

Lichfield Foundry

Walsall Foundry

HISTORY OF
CHAMBERLIN AND HILL

PART

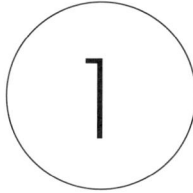

1

5

And so it begins
(1890 – 1896)

On a sunny day in the early spring of 1890, a small group of sleepy reddish-brown cows grazing in the field in Chuckery, Walsall, were a little alarmed by the sudden arrival of some unfamiliar and somewhat menacing looking men who rather brazenly walked around, talking at the top of their voices, pointing to something invisible ahead of them and disturbing the quiet idyll of the pasture. Had the chubby Herefords known what was to come, they would have been alarmed a great deal more. The plot that only sixteen years ago its owner, Lord Atherton, had sold to Mr William Cox, was to be sold again. The buyers, Messrs James Chamberlin and Henry Hill, had very different plans for this chunk of unspoiled rural retreat.

Look at the door handle

Several weeks later, even more people started arriving on the site. Endless horse-drawn carriages laden with bricks followed; soon the whole area was cleared of grass and all the creatures, big and small, living or feasting there. Trees were replaced by scaffolding. A massive building of considerable height and two slightly smaller ones slowly emerged from the ground. In a matter of months the pasture was turned into an industrial estate. The fate of the cattle remains unknown.

The Chuckery foundry, named after the area of Walsall where it now stood, began trading in 1890. It was founded by James Chamberlin, ex-salesman from Reading, who took charge of the production, and Henry Hill, former engineer from Foleshill, who was responsible for the sales. The Black Country, with its extensive supplies of coal, was a perfect location for such an enterprise. But the availability of furnace fuel was not the only advantage that came with this location. Birmingham, only fifteen miles away, was a bit of an anomaly on the industrial landscape of the country. Known as the "city of a thousand trades", it accommodated a great number of small factories and workshops churning out everything from guns and toys to stationery and cutlery. If you wanted to find a specific man-made object, you would have almost certainly found it in Birmingham and, if not, you could definitely have had it manufactured there. Hundreds of very different but interdependent small-scale producers, in tight cooperation with each other, were the driving force behind the phenomenal industrial success of Birmingham and its satellite towns, and reliably attracted highly skilled labourers to the area. The newly built foundry fitted perfectly within the highly-developed manufacturing infrastructure and was guaranteed to find the necessary number of competent employees. So the partners chose well.

Were they visionaries capable of analysing and predicting the prevailing patterns of the country's economy? Or were they simply lucky opportunists surfing on the wave-crest of the second industrial revolution? Probably a bit of both, but one thing is clear: it worked. Right from the beginning the company started generating profit which was reinvested into the business, enabling it to grow further. Together with the company grew the confidence and financial security of its founders. In the middle of 1893, James Chamberlin, evidently comfortable in his new role, travelled back to Reading to marry his fiancée, Edith Emma Pearton, and brought her to his newly purchased house in Sutton Road near the Chuckery. Henry

Hill had already moved his family to their new home in Lysway Street, ten minutes' walk away from the foundry. Now both partners were firmly established in Walsall.

The Chuckery was built to produce fine surface-finish cast iron castings. All sorts of domestic merchandise were made that way, and all of them bore a mark of outstanding craftsmanship. The following photographs, despite their somewhat substandard quality, demonstrate the elaborate patterns that adorn mundane household objects and turn them into pieces of art, however mass produced. Look at the door handle! Can you believe that it wasn't woven by a teenage flower fairy from weightless threads of silk somewhere at the edge of an enchanted forest? In fact, it was cast from molten iron in a hellishly hot foundry by a guy wiping sweat from his brow with his calloused hands. These intricate, lace-like patterns were possible to make due to a special technique that involved the use of "facing sand". To prepare it, different types of sand and some coal dust had been mixed together; then the whole blend was milled for about ten minutes. When poured into the mould, hot metal would burn off the coal, creating a thin layer of gas directly next to the surface of the pattern, delivering a smooth and delicate finish. In the era of total pteridomania, or "fern fever", that affected Victorians on both sides of the Pond, the ability of the heavy industry to reproduce the elegantly fine motifs of the plant's leaves, immortalising them in metal, would have been particularly valuable.

Such home furnishings, where the extreme durability of cast iron met the exquisite beauty of the design, were highly popular with consumers from all walks of life. Regardless of what rung of the social ladder one stood on, everybody strived to decorate the facade of their house, as well as its interior, with the highest degree of opulence that was within their means. Victorians took the curb appeal of their properties very seriously. A front door adorned with an ornamental knocker, handle or letterbox cover like the ones produced in Walsall, was meant, on behalf of its owner, to proudly proclaim: "Look, I can afford this!" In return, the founders kept polishing their skills, as if to say: "Look, I can make this!" Could this mutually-propelling desire to show off have been a positive force, instigating technological progress? Now that's a thought…

In 1896, when for the first time the account books of the company stated its net profit, it amounted to £2,336 which, according to the Bank of England Inflation Calculator, would be £314,000 in today's terms; in the following year it was £2,574, equivalent to £342,135 today. The business was booming. By now the volume of orders exceeded the capacity of the Chuckery. The only way to meet the demand was to expand the business. In the same year the partners began their search for the premises of a new foundry.

6

From malt to melt
(1896 – 1897)

B y 1896, the Chuckery was a regular supplier of castings to **Tuke and Bell Ltd**, a general engineering firm situated in the city of Lichfield. Building their next foundry on the doorstep of one of their larger customers seemed not only to provide a perfect solution to the capacity problem of the existing one, but also to significantly reduce transportation costs. Besides, at the turn of the century, due to its well-established railway links to northern parts of the kingdom, Lichfield was seen as "a gateway to the North", so starting production there would have opened up numerous possibilities for the expansion of the business well beyond the Black Country area. As usual, the partners' impeccable tactical thinking guaranteed a long-term strategic advantage.

The local government of Lichfield, however, did not share the enthusiasm of James Chamberlin and Henry Hill. According to the city's regulations, no properties of any kind were allowed to be built within two hundred yards of the cathedral, and the partners had to look for a suitable site just outside that radius. What they found was so much better than just a plot of land...

A disused brewery in Beacon Street in Lichfield had seen better days. Its buildings were still in a decent order, but the production had stopped being profitable a while ago, so by the 1890s it was nothing more than a non-functioning "blot on the landscape". And that was about to change.

When James Chamberlin came across the ex-brewery, it didn't take him long to realise that, in fact, he was looking at a ready-made foundry in need of some relatively small and inexpensive adjustments. The old brewery was never to deliver the thirst-quenching, cheer-inducing liquid ever again. Its almost empty three-storey building was large and, more importantly, had tall enough ceilings to accommodate the production of a totally different kind of fluid. It even had a hoist whose purpose was to lift malt, hops and other ingredients to the top floor where they were to be heated, and which, in its reincarnation as a part of a foundry, could be used for loading the cupola. The decision to rent the brewery must have been one of the easiest the partners had ever had to make: converting an existing construction of a suitable size into a foundry was a lot more cost effective than erecting one from scratch. The lease of the **Lichfield Brewery Co. Ltd**. to Chamberlin and Hill was completed on 13th of November 1896. According to the account books from the following year, it cost them £102 16s annually, or £13,690 in today's money. Was it worth it?

The new foundry, meaningfully named Phoenix, was not built to be a simple extension of the Chuckery. No delicately filigreed door knockers could be found on assembly lines here. It was configured to make larger castings for machine tools like parts of weaving devices, pedestal drills, lathes, milling machines and other instruments, similarly non-glamorous but essential for a wide range of industries and textile trade. Phoenix was producing and selling castings made to a customer's specifications and in most cases using the customer's drawings. Unlike the Chuckery in Walsall, which manufactured the company's own designs, Phoenix was created to fulfil specific orders of its clients. Both foundries functioned in parallel to each other with an equal degree of success. Over the next five years, the stated net profit for the company was £21,704, equivalent to £2,918,430 in today's terms. Managing this extremely efficient, ever-growing and attention-seeking organism was becoming more and more complicated, while both founders were not getting any younger. As often in life, their success came at a price: Henry Hill's health deteriorated, and he started to consider retirement in the very near future. It became clear that the management needed some reinforcement.

7

New kid on the block
(1897 – 1903)

B ut how can you find an adequate replacement for someone who, in the past fifteen years, had invested all his time, energy and finances into a business that carried not only his name but also his vision, his ideas and his understanding of both manufacturing and distribution of the product? How can you replace someone in possession of the deepest knowledge of the foundry, the knowledge that has been accumulated by generations of his family and seemed to be imprinted in his genome? Someone who had painstakingly created a strong net of connections and relationships within the industry? In short, to replace Henry Hill they needed to find a younger and fitter version of Henry Hill. And they needed him fast.

This was a task and a half. For weeks on end partners had been discussing possible candidates for the position, but none ticked all the boxes. Meanwhile, the pressing matters of the foundry took Henry Hill to the weighing machine factory that belonged to William and Thomas Avery. Weighing machines were comprised mainly of cast-iron parts, so in 1895, to the three plants it had already owned, W&T Avery added the famous Soho Foundry in Smethwick that used to belong to the legendary James Watt and Co. Chamberlin and Hill were one of W&T Avery's main suppliers; they made smaller castings required for the production of more complex units manufactured in Smethwick. During a routine discussion, Henry Hill mentioned the problem of his replacement to the manager of the factory, not realising that right at that moment he was facing the solution. Quite literally...

Henry Knollys Bather

This manager was twenty-four-year-old Herbert Knollys Bather, the fourth eldest son of John and Isabella Bather. John Bather was a wealthy farmer, owner of 230 acres of land in Shropshire. One of his nine children, Herbert knew that he had to make his own way in life and his own fortune.

Here is his portrait. In the photo, taken around the beginning of the twentieth century, we see a young man in his late thirties, looking trouble-free, attractive, sleek, even dandyish. Just for a moment, let's replace his immaculately groomed and pomaded hair with today's fashionable, if of questionable aesthetic value, faux hawk; change his perfectly trimmed moustache to weirdly contemporary beard in Van Dyke style; and swap his sharp three-piece-suit for a bomber jacket over a tee embellished with some mystifying slogan – and I can easily imagine him clenching a cup of organic matcha latte from Starbucks on his way to an office somewhere in town. What I struggle with is imagining him walking among swarms of fireflies of the non-biological variety on the shop floor stained with coal dust. Yet he was in charge of a large factory, and the factory was running like clockwork. Henry Hill must have been impressed by the energy, knowledge and organisational skills of Herbert Bather; more importantly, he must have recognised the ambition that was the latter's driving force. I suspect that, middle-aged and worn out, Henry Hill simply found in the factory manager what he had been looking for: his younger self. Which meant that Herbert Bather not only was a perfect candidate for Henry's replacement, but he also would have been keen to accept the challenge. (Much later, the Mayor of Lichfield would describe him as *"a very quiet man of a retiring nature"* who *"took very little part in public activities, devoting his whole energies to the development of his business".)*

Henry Hill was right. On the 11th April 1903, the following notice appeared in the Walsall Observer:

> *Notice is hereby given, that the partnership lately carried on by James William Chamberlin and Henry Hill under the style of Firm of "Chamberlin and Hill" at the Chuckery Foundry, Walsall and at the Phoenix Foundry, Lichfield, both in the County of Stafford, Ironfounders, was this day dissolved by mutual consent, as from the 1st day of January, 1903. The business will in future be carried on as a Joint-Stock Company under the style of "Chamberlin and Hill Ltd", and they will discharge all liabilities of the late firm.*
>> *Dated the 8th day of April, 1903.*
>>> *J.W. Chamberlin.*
>>> *Henry Hill.*
>> *Witness to the signatures of the said*
>> *J.W. Chamberlin and Henry Hill*
>> *David Davis - Solicitor, Birmingham.*

And, with that, the partnership that had lasted over a decade came to an end. Henry Hill's retirement deal was fused with Herbert Bather's arrangement to become a co-manager of the company alongside James Chamberlin. As part of the agreement, Hill was to receive £11,500 (£1,430,000 today) for his share of the business that included the transfer of the property in Scholefield Street (the japanning factory he had bought from one of Chamberlin's brothers-in-law prior to starting the enterprise). £3,000 of the pay-out came from Herbert Bather who, without looking back, invested all his savings into the business which he was determined, in time, to make his own. He negotiated the option of buying from Henry Hill all or part of his shares in the company within six years by giving one month's notice. At the same time, James Chamberlin consented to selling him, eventually, all the shares he then held. On the 3rd of March 1903, an agreement was made allowing Herbert Bather to purchase the business for the fixed price of £26,000. He was to draw an annual salary of £250 per year (just a little over £31,000 today), the same as his co-manager. All the surplus profits were to be devoted to buying James Chamberlin out. For the time being, the company was to continue under the joint management. On the 3rd of April 1903, Chamberlin & Hill became a Limited Company. Immediately, they took out a mortgage of £10,000 and five days later purchased two more plots of land in Chuckery in order to expand the original foundry.

Now things were really looking up.

8

And then there was none
(1904 – 1913)

H erbert Bather's transition to Chamberlin and Hill seemed to have happened seamlessly. The profits of the company continued to grow, and its managers' plans were bigger still. There was every reason to be optimistic about the future. However, on the 10th of January 1904, the otherwise bright horizon was clouded by sad news: on that day Henry Hill passed away at his home in Lysway Street. He was fifty-nine years old and must have been suffering from ill health for a while, and yet his death came as a shock. One of the two men who, at their own risk, created and set in motion this now perfectly functioning mechanism, was no longer there. His name, though, was fused into that of the company. And not just his name. The Hill family still had shares in the business, and Henry's daughter Agnes Barbara, the second eldest out of four, who from the very beginning had been keeping the company's books in her impeccable handwriting issuing the invoices and statements to the customers, was to continue working for her father's enterprise for many years to come.

The new managerial tandem carried on. The profit in 1904 was £2,596; in 1905 it reached £2,946, corresponding to today's £322,797 and £366,318 respectively. The time had come to expand the business again. On the 4th of May 1905, the grounds and buildings of the Phoenix, that previously had been rented from the Lichfield Brewery, were bought outright together with an adjacent chunk of land in Beacon Street in order to extend the foundry even further. Now **Chamberlin and Hill Ltd** owned both the Walsall and Lichfield sites.

It would be equally wrong and unfair to continue describing the success of the company concentrating purely on the "upstairs" part of it. What about the hundreds of workmen who spent ten hours a day six days a week making all this happen? Without them, neither massive investments nor clever management would have turned tons of shapeless bits of ore into millions of cast iron gadgets and utensils needed by households and factories in the country.

The problem is, this story is based on the company's archives and on personal conversations. A century separating me from the actual participants of the events ruled out the possibility of chatting with them, and all the remaining documents, being reflective of the zeitgeist, contain no information about the people on the "shop floor". But this doesn't mean that the efforts of the employees were not appreciated by their employers. Herbert Bather was keen to demonstrate his gratitude to his workers. Here is a short article from the Walsall Observer in August 1905:

> *"A Party in connection with the employees of Messrs. Chamberlin and Hill, Chuckery Foundry, Walsall, and Phoenix Foundry Lichfield, was held on Saturday in the beautiful grounds of Mr H K Bather's Moat Bank home, near Lichfield. Dinner and tea were provided, and the tent and tables were very tastefully decorated. During the afternoon, the workmen enjoyed the sports, and after tea, Mr Bather distributed prizes to the winners of various events."*

In 1907 James Chamberlin, confident in Herbert Bather's ability to run the business, decided to step down from his position. He no longer received his salary but was paid a £5 Director's fee for the attendance of board meetings. His place in the management team was taken by one of the shareholders, Robert Buchanan. After 1907, Chamberlin's name was no longer mentioned in the business's books. He continued to hold a significant number of shares until, around 1912, Herbert Knollys Bather fulfilled his obligation of paying for them in full. After that it appears that James Chamberlin left the company for good. From then on, both of the founders of **Chamberlin and Hill Ltd** were present by name only.

The full change of the management did not slow down the growth of the business. Over the next six years, its profits reached £15,850 (£1,850,408 today), and more workers were required to keep up with the ever increasing levels of production. Jobs were frequently advertised in local newspapers, attracting a lot of interest: the company offered supplementary weekly wages to allow the trainees to have reasonable income while they were still learning. The vacancies filled quickly.

Manufacturing children's toys proved to be a very profitable affair. Authentic looking toy guns like the one pictured here sold particularly well. From the lofty height of 2022 we can see to what extent this naive "pretend brutality" was infused with a sinister prophesying symbolism: those guns were a very popular Christmas present for boys in the run-up to the year 1914.

Toy gun manufactured in 1914

Supplement to Part I:
Simply statistics

YEAR	SALES	COST OF PRODUCTION	% OF SALES	COST OF DISTRIBUTION	% OF SALES	TRADING PROFIT	% OF PROFIT ON SALES
1911	£17,600.72	£11,014.66	62.58%	£3,947.42	22.43%	£2,638.64	14.99%
1912	£18,525.69	£11,554.55	62.37%	£4,299.55	23.21%	£2,671.59	14.42%
1913	£18,653.59	£11,564.13	61.99%	£4,154.66	22.27%	£2,934.80	15.73%
1914	£18,575.75	£11,519.98	62.02%	£4,278.95	23.04%	£2,776.82	14.95%
1915	£13,017.84	£8,013.37	61.56%	£3,249.55	24.96%	£1,754.92	13.48%
1916	£17,655.99	£9,699.90	54.94%	£2,781.94	15.76%	£5,174.15	29.31%
1917	£19,834.65	£11,989.43	60.45%	£3,983.83	20.09%	£3,861.39	19.47%
1918	£28,219.36	£15,617.40	55.34%	£4,926.36	17.46%	£7,675.60	27.20%
1919	£30,021.31	£17,536.97	58.42%	£5,734.96	19.10%	£6,749.38	22.48%
1920	£38,008.42	£20,920.13	55.04%	£7,065.15	18.59%	£10,023.14	26.37%
1921	£64,007.08	£37,846.67	59.13%	£10,936.97	17.09%	£15,223.44	23.78%
1922	£24,930.08	£13,520.17	54.23%	£5,997.53	24.06%	£5,412.38	21.71%
1923	£23,829.40	£13,042.66	54.73%	£6,079.97	25.51%	£4,706.77	19.75%

Data From Heathcote and Coleman 1923

HISTORY OF
CHAMBERLIN AND HILL

PART

2

9

"The isle of saints and soldiers"
(1914 – 1916)

This must be running in the family. I mean the Hominidae family. The insane desire to use the same object as a tool for creating something and as a weapon for destroying that very thing, together with its creator, has been a constant and universal feature of every human civilization that we know of. Humans have spent 3,132 out of 3,400 years of their recorded history in violent conflicts of various magnitudes. The Great War that broke out in July 1914 happened to be the deadliest one to date. The Industrial Revolution had obligingly provided the European nations with weaponry of unmatched power and killing potential, producing it on an unprecedented scale. Henry Ford's ingenious innovation, the assembly line, delivered parts of automobiles and parts of tanks with equally impartial readiness. The newest device in the military toolbox, the machine gun, changed combat forever. Never before had it been possible to take so many lives with so little effort.

The news from the trenches was devastating, and this triggered feelings of defiance and camaraderie, and a surge of patriotic fervour in those left behind the lines. Even though Chamberlin and Hill Foundries, as part of the iron and steel industries, were exempt from call-up, a lot of their workers joined the armed forces. We don't know the exact number of those who walked away from the heat of the furnace straight into the heat of the battle. But we do know that there were many, and their bravery matched their diligence. Here is a cutting from the *Staffordshire Advertiser* dated 8th of December 1917:

MILITARY MEDALLIST

Sergeant Frederick Taylor, North Staffordshire Regiment, youngest son of Mr Thomas Taylor, Netherstowe, Lichfield, has been awarded the Military Medal for bravery on the battlefield. The conduct for which he earned the decoration is described as follows: Sergeant Taylor took his platoon up to the front to assist another platoon that was held up. Having broken through and taken the position, Sergeant Taylor crawled over the top, under machine gun fire, to some wounded in a shell hole and got them to safety: otherwise, they would have lost their lives. In a letter received by his wife, who lives in Beacon Street Lichfield, his superior officer says: "Your husband is a man to be proud of, the coolest and bravest I have ever met. You are lucky to possess such a husband as I am to possess such a non-commissioned officer".

*Sergeant Taylor was formerly employed at
Messer's Chamberlin and Hill's Iron foundry.
Beacon Street, Lichfield.*

Meanwhile, the company was expected to switch their usual production to munition: the monstrous war machine needed constant fuelling. **Chamberlin and Hill Ltd** had to make castings for hand grenades and six-inch Howitzers, a type of field gun. The problem of meeting the ever-increasing demand with the ever-diminishing number of workmen had only one solution.

On 15th of December 1916, *The Lichfield Mercury* printed the following advertisement on its "Jobs" page:

TO MUNITION WORKERS.

We are requested by the Ministry of Munitions to introduce FEMALE LABOUR into our FOUNDRY for the increased production of Munitions.

We are anxious to know how far such labour is available.

The work is heavy, and none but strong hefty women are any use. Furthermore they would have to wear trousers and strong boots.

All prices are arranged on a piecework basis, and in default of any experience it is impossible now to state any fixed rates of pay; but the men are making big money and there is no reason why women should not do well.

If any women are desirous of assisting us, I shall be pleased to meet them on Monday Afternoon, at 3 o'clock, at our Beacon Street Foundry and show them what I can.

In any case we could not make a start before January 1st, 1917.

CHAMBERLIN & HILL, LTD.,

H. K. BATHER,

Director.

Beacon Street Foundry,

14th December, 1916. Lichfield.

Women Workers Wanted

At first glance it appears that Herbert Bather was less than keen on the idea of employing female workers in his foundries. *"We are requested by the Ministry of Munitions"* begins the ad, as if to allow the company to distance itself from such a decision. I can't help reading between the lines: *"Watch out, ladies! The job is so hard that only those resembling a circus weight-lifter need bother applying!"* But if we thought that Herbert Knollys Bather was a misogynist who, under normal circumstances, would have never allowed women into his foundries, we couldn't be further from the truth.

Here is another advertisement published in the *Walsall Observer* on 12th of March, nearly four months before the beginning of the war: "*Woman wanted to take charge of plating shop…*" It was a challenging job even if not as physically demanding as the ones in the foundry because it involved dealing with dangerous chemicals like cyanide. Whoever did it needed to know what she (or he) was doing.

I believe that Herbert Bather did not object to women working for the company; instead, he was understandably concerned with finding the candidates who were physically capable of doing the job that even men considered hard. What's more, he offered women the same wage as their male counterparts: a move highly unusual in 1916 and not always popular with employers even today, over a century later!

In the absence of men who had left for the trenches, women's involvement in industrial production became crucial. As the French Field Marshal and Commander-in-Chief Joseph Joffre put it, "*if the women in the factories stopped work for twenty minutes, the Allies would lose the war*".

They evidently didn't stop.

We don't have any documents showing the number of women working in C&H foundries in the course of the war. Nor do we know exactly how many pieces of munition, produced by women, left the gates of the foundries during these years. But it's difficult to imagine that without female contribution to the work of the foundries the company would have met the high demands of the industry and achieved such a substantial financial gain. The figures that Gordon found in the company's archive speak for themselves: in 1916 alone, the profit was £9,293 which, after a levy of £4,099, left C&H with £5,662 in the bank. The trend remained unchanged in the following years.

This levy, a sort of a temporary tax of 50% (later going up to 80%) on excess profits, i.e. profits above a pre-war standard for the same accounting period, was placed on businesses by Swedish and Danish governments in early 1915, and by the end of that year fifteen more countries, including Britain, did the same. The money raised in that way was used to fund the war efforts, and later it would be invested into the economic recovery of the country as a whole. Between 1916, when the levy was first applied, and 1920 when it was scrapped, C&H contributed £24,705 (over £46,836,714 today) to the needs of the country in the levy alone. Like other businesses, they also issued a war loan to the government as well as Exchequer Bonds.

And yet, despite the toughest economic conditions possible, in 1920 the company's account at the Midland Bank in Walsall registered £9,867 (£450,996).

At the end of the war the company found itself in an even better financial situation than before July 1914. Would it be fair to think that thousands of hand grenades manufactured by C&H, each of them possibly responsible for dozens of deaths – deaths of the enemy, but human deaths nevertheless – were the reason for the financial success of the company? Or was the opposite true: munitions produced in the foundries supported British soldiers in combat, becoming, in fact, life-saving devices and, at the same time, bringing the company its well-deserved reward? What is the right way of looking at it? And is there a right way?

10

"Where have all the flowers gone?"
(1916 – 1926)

A single bullet, seven grams of lead encased in a soft steel jacket shot by the Serbian Gavrilo Princip from a Belgian-made semi-automatic pistol, went right through the neck of the Archduke of Austria Franz Ferdinand, killing the heir to the Austro-Hungarian throne and, having ricocheted from the wall of global political tensions, caused an unstoppable avalanche of identical lumps of deadly metal that swept over more than a hundred countries, turning peaceful grounds into battlefields and taking millions of lives: cruelly, eagerly, indiscriminately.

On 23rd of April 1916, in the early evening, Edith Emma and James William Chamberlin received the crushing news: their only son, Private John Pearson Chamberlin, 14th Battalion of the Royal Warwickshire Regiment, had been killed in battle at Pozieres Ridge. The night he died, his regiment undertook the first attempt to capture the high grounds of Pozieres Ridge on the Albert-Bapaume Road during the now infamous Battle of the Somme. The joint forces of the British and the Australians fought against the Germans for the observation point overlooking the surrounding countryside. Private Chamberlin, whom everybody called Jack, was nineteen years old. He would find his final resting place at Caterpillar Valley Memorial, Lingaeval, France. His father would never visit his grave.

James William Chamberlin outlived Jack by less than four years and died on 6th of March 1920, just before his son's reburial. He was fifty-eight years old and in reasonably good health.

The Chamberlins were not the only family connected to the company to suffer such a loss. After hours of looking through the local newspapers' archives, Gordon Stanley came across a few more names in the obituary columns. Here are these little articles, word-by-word:

WIESMOOR SOLDIER FALLS AT GALLIPOLI

To the list of local soldiers who have given their lives fighting for Britain on the Gallipoli Peninsula, must be added the name of Private Thomas Daniel Merriman (22) of 6 Hateley's Lane, Wisemore, who, according to the War Office notice, fell while in action with the 7th North Stafford's some six weeks ago. Prior to Joining the Army twelve months ago was a caster and formerly worked for Chamberlin & Hill of Chuckery. His widow is left with one child. Aged fifteen months, the baby being a few days old when the deceased enlisted.

(Walsall Observer, 17th Sept 1915).

QUEEN STREET SOLDIER TWICE WOUNDED

Although he served through the South African Campaign without injury, Private Arthur Boffy, of 163 Queen Street, Pleck, has not been so fortunate in this war, for he has been twice wounded and is now in Hospital. Recovering from his first injury, he had only just re-joined his battalion, the 3rd Royal Warwick's, in the firing line about a week when he was wounded a second time through the left lung. He is unmarried and about thirty-three years of age, and when called up on reserve was in the employ of Messrs Chamberlin & Hill.

(Walsall Observer, 20th Jan 1917).

PRIVATE THOMAS BLEWITT

Whose brother whose death is reported above, has been killed in action, is officially reported to have died in France on April 15 from wounds received while in action with the South Stafford's two days previously, aged 26 and a single man, he enlisted in October 1914, and has served in France for over three years, during which time he has been wounded twice and recovered. His home was at 52, Badla Street, and he was formerly employed by Messrs Chamberlin & Hill, Chuckery Road.

(Walsall Observer, April 27th 1918).

Is this the full list of C&H foundry men who gave their lives in the battles of the Great War? We don't know. But whether complete or not, it is too long. Four names too long.

The ruthless bullet that had gone on the killing spree in Sarajevo in 1914 finally stopped its murderous rounds. The battlefields went back to being just fields. In the following spring they were covered in poppies, red like the blood that had soaked the soil on which they grew. The human desire to assign some meaning to every event created the beautifully poetical interpretation of this fact: nature itself seemed to be grieving together with people, remembering the casualties of the war.

But in reality the explanation of the botanical mystery is very prosaic. The explosions of combat disturbed the poppy seeds that had been lying dormant in the soil for dozens of years, nudging them to propagate. Nature simply took its course.

There is no poetry in war.

II

Herbert Bather Instead
of Herbert Bather
(1927 – 1938)

In 1927, at the age of 64, Herbert Bather, now the solo owner of C&H Ltd, was ready for retirement. Unlike the founders of the company, he didn't need to look far for his own replacement. His eldest son was keen to take over.

Born in 1903, Herbert Fiennes, in keeping with the tradition of the time, inherited the first name from his father and the middle name from his maternal grandfather, Lieutenant General Fiennes Middleton Colville, a soldier of high reputation who went on to receive a knighthood. In addition to his first name, he inherited a place on the board of C&H, which he joined at the age of twenty-four becoming its Managing Director. His father stayed on as the chairman. Both of them continued to work together while young Herbert was learning the secrets of successful management from Herbert Knollys. They made a good team, and the results of their cooperation can be seen in the figures of the company performance: the total sales in 1928 were £29,465 with net profits of £4,073; in 1929 they were, respectively, £26,567 and £3,682. By then, for nearly a decade, the foundries had been producing an extensive range of simple domestic necessities that would have been used in households throughout the country every single day: trivets, corkscrews, can openers, potato mashers – the list can go on. Items manufactured by C&H might have been ordinary, but the designs were elaborate as ever, turning mundane objects into beautiful artefacts, bringing a little glamour into monotonous routine. This strategy explained to a great extent the high volume of sales. Herbert Knollys Bather was satisfied with his son's ability to steer the company in the right direction. In 1929, he took full retirement and did what a lot of well-off pensioners choose to do: went travelling. In the passenger listing of the ship going to Kenya and then further on to South Africa, his profession was stated as "none".

His "life of leisure" didn't last long. On 23rd of October 1933 the following report appeared in *The Staffordshire Advertiser*:

> *"Mr Herbert Knollys Bather, aged 70, a retired iron founder of Lichfield, died in tragic circumstances. Mr Bather was shooting at Walton-on-Trent... when he became ill and died almost immediately... He was succeeded by his two daughters, Dorothy Colville and Mary Helen, and his two sons, George Northcote and Herbert Fiennes."*

The last of the three men who had laid the foundation of Chamberlin and Hill, was gone. The business was to continue.

And it did. Herbert Fiennes shared his father's ability to run the company in the most efficient way. Profits continued to grow, possibly except for the period between 1929 and 1932. I have to say "possibly" because we don't have figures for these years. Among other account books kept in the archive of C&H was a heavy reddish-brown leather-bound volume, worn around the edges, looking important and mysterious, like a sorcerer's manual. And it was locked. A massive brass hasp fixed across the pages was not a decoration but a proper lock with a keyhole – and no key in sight. The book contained the accounts for the time of the Great Depression when the Gross Domestic Product had fallen by fifteen per cent in most countries. Presumably, in those economic conditions, C&H suffered a similar blow. In June 1931 the company was in need of raising some money, so a patch of land near the corner of Beacon Street and Chuckery Road was placed for an auction which must have allowed them to stay true to their motto: *"We have always generated a profit in every year of trade."* But we will never know the details: Gordon was too much of a gentleman to pick the lock of the enigmatic book.

By the end of 1931, the country began to recover from the crisis. British goods were becoming more competitive on the global market. In the Midlands the effects of the Depression were particularly short lived. C&H was back on track. The ordinary, lock-free accounts books demonstrate the rate of the company's success in the post-Depression years: net profit in the period 1935 to 1938 was £31,742 (£2,184,908 today).

Britain's economic recovery was accompanied by an array of innovations slowly finding their way into people's lives: the national grid, the first of its kind in the world, delivered to homes electricity and all the perks that come with it; the first washing machine and vacuum cleaner appeared on the market, promising to simplify tedious daily chores in many households; television broadcasts became a regular affair; British-made cars flooded the roads, accelerating the introduction of the Highway Code while speeding up. Sitting behind the wheel, drivers cursed the newly imposed thirty mph limit and crooned verses from one of the most popular hits of the decade, "Let's face the music and dance": "*there may be trouble ahead…*"

12

"Keep calm and carry on"
(1939 – 1945)

"There may be trouble ahead" happened to be a prescient line: for a while, the trouble, indeed, had been brewing deep within the international scene and was about to break through the fragile shell of the young peace. Military conflicts erupted in all corners of the world, but the main disaster, yet again, was to come from Europe: in the West, a pale, thin man with a moustache resembling a bird dropping that had landed on his top lip, and a long strand of thinning hair seemingly glued to his forehead, was planning to undertake a global racial cleansing and establish a new world order under the rule of the German "master race"; in the East, a short stocky man with a bushier moustache, fuller hair but equally dark soul, was dreaming of creating a new world order of a different kind, turning the planet into his own unified communist empire. Führer struck just before Comrade had a chance.

The Great War which had ended only two decades ago and which, at the time, was considered the deadliest of all human conflicts, would prove to be no more than a dress rehearsal for World War Two which began on 1st of September 1939 as the consequence of Hitler's forces invading Poland.

History, lacking imagination, was repeating itself, but on an even larger scale. Again, like over twenty years ago, men were leaving their homes, their families and jobs, including the jobs in industries exempt from conscription, to join the army. And again, the foundries of C&H had to switch to the production of castings to support the war effort. Again they were making hand grenade castings as well as supplying parts to other industries involved in manufacturing munitions. Here are some of the companies that relied on **Chamberlin and Hill Ltd** in their daily operations: **Girling Ltd**, producer of braking components; **Sangamo Weston Ltd**, manufacturer of aircraft instruments; **Myford Engineering**, experts in making lathes, millers and drillers required for machining components; and **Frederic Pollard** with a similar range of products. **Rolls Royce Ltd Crewe**, manufacturing tanks and armoured vehicles on their Belper site, and **Perkins Engines**, who were building air-sea rescue launchers, are also on that list.

The workload was formidably high, while the number of people who could do it was dramatically reduced. The help came from an unexpected place.

After the declaration of war, all 70,000 German, Austrian and Italian residents of the UK had been classed as "enemy aliens". Suspected of being part of the "fifth column", they were put through trials; as the result of those, thousands of foreign nationals were arrested and sent to internment camps across the UK. However, to ease the pressure on British manufacturers, a number of those, including C&H, were given an opportunity to employ some of the internees. This is how a group of Italian men came to work in both Chuckery and Phoenix. They received basic training and were allowed to live close to the foundry. (No documented evidence is left of their performance or the way they fitted in, but it must have been a success: after the end of the war, the company's Managing Director wrote to the Ministry of Employment asking for permission for those ex-internees to stay in the country if they wished to do so. The permission was granted. As a result, many Italians chose to remain in the UK and continued working for C&H.)

These new workers took the place of all the volunteers who had joined the army and who, being used to the harsh conditions of the foundry, were endlessly inventive, knowing how to be constantly alert in the presence of danger: a skill that would have been indispensable in the trenches and would have saved the lives of many. Many, not all. Devastating messages kept appearing in the local newspapers. Here are the ones that Gordon managed to find:

From *Walsall Worker* October 21st 1944.

ARNHEM MAN WHO DID NOT RETURN.

Private Benjamin Bliss.

Mr and Mrs Bliss of 48, Chuckery Road, Walsall, received news last weekend that their son, Private Benjamin Bliss (aged 20) of the Royal Army Medical Corps. The Paratrooper had been posted Missing in Northwest Europe from Sept 23. Before he was called up in December 1942, he was employed by Chamberlin and Hill, and was an old boy of Chuckery School. The father of Private Bliss served with a Highland Regiment in the last war.

From *Walsall Observer* October 21st 1944.

Lichfield workers

An official telegram conveying the sad news of the death in action near Cassino, Italy of their elder son Lieutenant Frederick Warren Taylor, of the Royal Artillery, was received on Friday evening by Captain and Mrs G. F. Taylor, Headmaster and Matron of Beacon Residential School, Beacon Street Lichfield. "Freddie" as the deceased officer was familiarly known to his many friends, was aged 25 years of age. Upon leaving school he was employed by Messrs Chamberlin and Hill Ltd., Ironfounders, Lichfield. In May 1939, he joined the Lichfield Territorials, and later became a sergeant in the intelligence section of the North Staffs Regiment. After obtaining his commission in 1942 he went with the R.A. to the Shetland Isles.

He has recently been in the fighting in Italy and took part in the original battle of Cassino, in the vicinity of which he evidently met his Death. Mr and Mrs Taylor have been the recipients of numerous expressions of sympathy in the very great loss they have sustained.

About 18 months ago the engagement was announced between Lt. Taylor and Miss Betty Norman, of King's Bromley. Who has also received messages of condolence from a wide circle of friends.

A memorial service for the deceased officer will take place at St. Chad's Church, Lichfield, tomorrow (Saturday), at 2.30 p.m.

From *Lichfield Mercury* September 8th 1944.
Lance Corporal George Wolfe.

In the "Mercury" of August 18, we published extracts from a letter received by his parents from L/Cpl George White, North Staffordshire Regiment, paying tribute to the fighting qualities of the local lads who were upholding the good name and traditions of the North Stafford's, and concluding: " I don't want you to worry over me. I am confident of coming through and having that great reunion party – and what a party it will be."

L/Cpl Wolfe did not live to receive that issue of the "Mercury" for on Saturday last his parents received the Official intimation that he was killed in action in France on August 15th.

L/Cpl Wolfe who was 25 years of age, was the third son of Mr and Mrs J Wolfe of 24, Sandford Street, Lichfield, and he leaves a young widow and a two-year-old daughter who reside at 188, Beacon Street. He was a Lichfield Territorial before the war and during his five years war service he served in Ireland, the Orkneys, and Shetlands, and for eight weeks in France. From the time he left school to the outbreak of war he was employed by Messrs: Chamberlin and Hill, Beacon Street. And was a playing member of their football club.

Bad news was coming not only from the front line.

In 1942, Agnes Barbara Williams, Henry Hill's daughter, took ill and had to retire from the company her father had built. She had worked there for nearly half a century. Agnes Barbara passed away on 23rd December 1943. Herbert Knollys Bather had described her once as "the most loyal and unselfish colleague"; at the funeral his son Herbert Fiennes spoke fondly about her: "She held the admiration, respect, and love of every member of the firm, and all feel that they have lost a friend, one who can never be adequately replaced." Little did anybody know that only a year later a heart-felt speech would be delivered at his own funeral.

On 13th of May 1944, Herbert Fiennes Bather went on to the foundry and didn't like what he saw. It was a Saturday, but the owner of the company didn't consider this a reason for not turning up at work. A great number of bags ready for shipping were in total disarray all over the floor of the dispatch bay. He spent the morning with the staff of the bay organising the bags, and then summoned Edward Harold Page, the man who had been hired in preparation for Agnes Barbara's retirement and who was responsible, among other things, for the smooth running of the dispatch department, instructing him to maintain high standards in the future. At lunchtime, he set out for his home in Lichfield but decided to stop at Phoenix to tidy up the dispatch bay there as well. Having completed the work, he went to his office to take a break. He never came out. Unexpectedly, like his father, Herbert Fiennes died aged only 41.

The company was now left without any form of management at the top level. It's impossible to know whether they were calm, but carry on they did, and they did it successfully. At the end of that year the net profit reached £9,718, and the market value of the investments was £37,408. C&H had passed the endurance test.

So had the whole country. The 8th of May 1945 marked the end of the war. The United Kingdom celebrated the victory. On that unforgettable Tuesday, the streets of Walsall, a brave little town which, over the past years, had lived and worked through bombings, tragic news from the front, food rationing and just incredible hardship, shed their cautiously grey, neutral appearance and blossomed with colourful flags and portraits of the Allied leaders. Joy was returning to Walsall together with spontaneous street parties, processions and bonfires. A thanksgiving service was held at the parish church. That evening, darkness was cancelled. The forecourt of the Council House was flooded with light and dancing people. A large, brightly illuminated cartoon-style image of Winston Churchill, mounted on a raft in the middle of Arboretum Lake, shone over the waters symbolising hope and promising the beginning of a new era, free of military conflict, destruction and suffering.

Meanwhile, Winston Churchill (the man, not the picture over the lake) was determined to make that promise come true. In 1946, in his "Speech to the academic youth" delivered at the University of Zurich he called for the creation of a "United States of Europe", starting a chain of events that years later would lead to the emergence of the European Union with the aim of ending the perpetual hostilities between European nations and preventing the Second World War from turning, like its predecessor, into a dress rehearsal of a next, even larger disaster leading to the final curtain call.

Supplements to Part II:
Simply statistics

(Some figures on the company's performance in this period)

CAPITAL

Authorised.	12,000 5% (free of income tax)	
	Cumulative Preference Shares, £1 each	12,000
	10,000 5% (free of income tax)	
	Cumulative Preference Shares, £1 each	10,000
	20,000 ordinary shares, £1 each	20,000

Debentures. 10,000. 5% Debentures have been redeemed; no outstanding debentures or mortgage debt.

Goodwill.   Goodwill has been written off.

NET PROFITS

(Net profits after the Managing Director's salary, fees and depreciation, income tax, excess profit duty and corporation profits tax, but before charging interest on debentures since redeemed)

Year to 31.03.	1920.	£4,072
Ditto.	1921.	£4,643
	1922.	£2.207
	1923.	£1,771
	1924.	£3,614
	1925.	£5,763
	1926.	£4,740
	1927.	£3,230+

Net profit average for 8 years –
£3,755 per annum (£233,456 today)

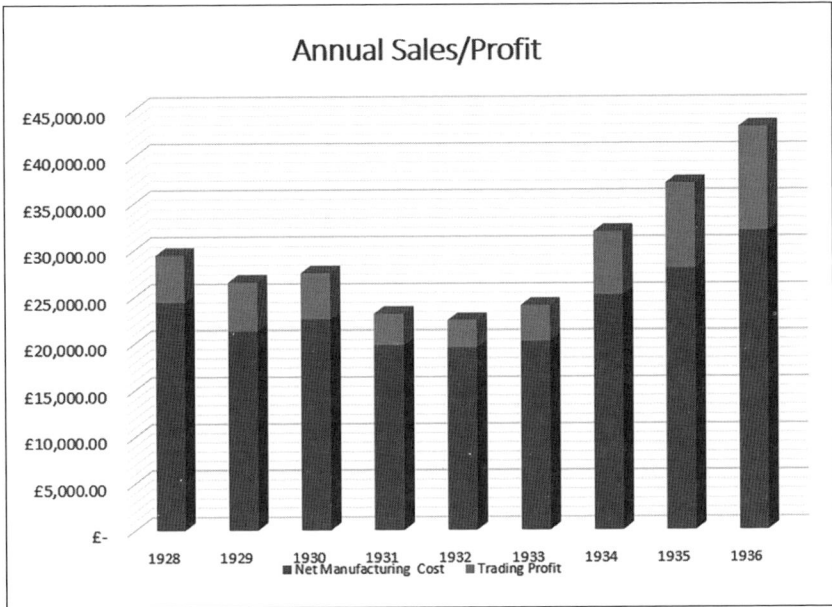

Annual Sales/Profit

Faces behind the headlines

Who were these men, going to the front straight from the foundry gate? Gordon Stanley, my guide and mentor in all matters foundry-related, comes from the dynasty of C&H employees. His father and uncles did exactly that: left their jobs at Chuckery to join the armed forces during the Second World War. Gordon's memoirs give us a rare opportunity to know a bit more about the real lives of the people who are often mentioned in newspaper reports and history books as no more than a name or even just a number. Remember lines like "The British army strength stood at 797,000 men"? Well, this is what a few of those faceless and nameless thousands were like, as remembered by a close relative. Here are a couple of pages from Gordon's memoirs:

> "In the early years all castings were made using the snapflask moulding method, with a hand squeeze machine by approximately 130 moulders. Among those were my father and his brothers. My uncle John Thomas Stanley, my father's eldest brother, born in 1915 and always known as "Jack", was the first of the brothers to join Chamberlin & Hill in the late 1920s. He would not fit in with the typical perception of a foundry worker. In his spare time,

after a day's hard work in the foundry, Jack would don his suit and patent leather shoes and take part in a ballroom formation dance team, dancing with a partner named Pearl Carrington. The team was well-known, winning a lot of medals. Despite his working background, Jack would come across as very well-spoken but he over-emphasised his H's; because of this, his nickname in the foundry was "Stinker", named after a "Posh" character of one of the B.B.C. Radio broadcasts. Although he was in a reserved occupation, Jack signed up for the Royal Navy and returned to the foundry after World War 2. Just to add to his character: many years later, in the 1960s, Jack went to help the operator, who was new to the job, when one of the cupolas would not open. Unknown to everyone, molten metal was gathered in the well in the bottom. As soon as Jack used a sledgehammer to remove the crossbar, the metal dropped, and he was standing up to his ankles in hot metal. A colleague lifted him quickly and saved his life. Despite the prognosis from the doctors that he would have difficulties walking, Jack was walking again within six months and not long afterwards playing golf.

The next brother to join the company was my father, Clarence William Stanley, born in 1916 and known as "Cal". Early in his teens, before leaving school, he got his first job at a local butcher's, in Park Street, Walsall, in their abattoir and worked on a Friday afternoon and all-day Saturday. At that time, the animals were brought to the butcher's shop and slaughtered there and then. He had to clear and clean the animals' carcase. Much later in his life, he told me how difficult it had been to hear the cries of a lamb slaughtered. Dad didn't think that he would have been able to do that part of the job... Luckily, he didn't have to. His payment was all the offal from one beast, which would keep his younger brothers and sisters in meals for a few days. After leaving school in the early 1930s, he joined his brother at Chamberlin & Hill. Like Jack, he worked as a moulder, which entailed producing moulds on a hand-squeeze machine, laying rows of moulds down onto the floor in front of their moulding station, ready for casting. When metal was available, it was distributed in a bucket-shaped container with a refractory lining called a shank by a continuous overhead gantry to moulders. They cast their moulds, leave them to cool down, and throw them in, separating castings from spent sand. This process would continue throughout the day when they would produce between 100 and 130 moulds depending upon the moulder's skill, stamina, size of the mould, and availability of metal. They would also collect the freshly milled facing sand, re-ganister their ladle, place it in an oven to cure the lining, and finally get into the showers to remove the dirt and sweat from their days' efforts. He would walk into the town centre where the family lived, and on these walks, he met a young lady who worked at J. A. Crabtree Electrical at the opposite end of Beacon Street. He tried his chat-up line, but she ignored him. He kept trying, and after a couple of days of walking alongside, they finally got talking, which is how he met my mother. Like his brother, dad signed up to join the armed forces, joining the Royal Artillery. He was stationed in the Orkney Isles on anti-aircraft guns protecting naval ships from German bombers in Scapa flow. Towards the end of the war, he was transferred onto the forts in the Solent to cover enemy planes attacking the naval dockyards of Portsmouth.

Also in the early 1930s, Clifford Verdun Stanley, "Cliff" to his workmates, started working for Chamberlin and Hill and also learned the moulding trade. He was born in 1918. Cliff also signed up at the beginning of the war to join the Armed forces. He met his future wife while based on the Isle of Wight. They got married in 1951 and had a son, Colin. Soon after Cliff returned to Walsall and Chamberlin & Hill, where he worked until 1953. The recently married couple decided to join many English families that emigrated to Australia after the war, as a £10 "Pommie", an Australian assisted scheme to encourage 'Brits' to set up home there. With Colin's help he built his own home in Perth, and an Electoral register later shows that he changed his occupation to a Bricklayer. Eventually he settled down in South Africa to live out the rest of his days.

Ernest Henry Arnold Stanley, "Ernie", born 1921, followed in the footsteps of his brothers. Ernie's childhood was marred by a road accident: at the age of three, he ran across the road and was hit by a horse pulling a cart. The horse's foot hit him on the side of the head-splitting his eyebrow and damaging his sight in one eye. Later, he had a problem hearing on the side of the injury. Like the other three brothers, he joined the team of Snapflask Moulders. At that time, good money could be earned, provided you were willing to work hard, and the Stanley brothers were willing to do that. He joined the armed forces in the war but not in a frontline position due to his disabilities, and re-joined the C&H foundry workers at Walsall after the war.

The Stanley family were lucky, with all the family members that joined the armed forces returning home uninjured.

Next to join the growing family team of moulders was Joseph Henry Stanley, "Joe", who was always said to be "a bit of a lad" even as a youngster, but always willing to help others. He started work at Chamberlin and Hill in the 1940s. Joe's call to join the forces was after the end of the war and would be by conscription. Joe served in the Royal Electrical and Mechanical Engineers, serving predominantly in India. He had several interesting hobbies: winemaking, working an allotment growing prize onions and leeks, breeding Chinchillas, and playing several musical instruments. Like most of C&H's foundrymen, Joe frequented the Chuckery Mutual Club at the end of the working day, to "lay the dust" (a term used for the several pints of beer that men drunk to swill down the dust breathed in during the working day) before going home. Joe would often play darts while having his odd pint, and on one occasion reached the finals of the News of the World Darts Championship, the championship every darts player wanted to win."

HISTORY OF
CHAMBERLIN AND HILL

PART

3

13

A problem shared is a problem…
split into 38,000 bits!
(1946 – 1950)

On 14th of May 1946, the *Birmingham Gazette* published its usual daily update on the Birmingham Stock Exchange. The long list of businesses featured in that particular issue included, for the first time ever, **Chamberlin and Hill Ltd.** With 38,000 shares at five shillings each offered to potential investors, C&H became a public company.

The chain of events preceding this move started two years prior, with the sudden death of the sole owner of the company, Herbert Fiennes Bather. Christina, his widow, to whom he had bequeathed all the shares, turned overnight from "a lady of leisure" into a proprietor of a business supplying the army with castings for munitions in war time. She didn't know much about the specifics of the industry. She was well off, but, apart from her home, all of her wealth was locked in a handful of buildings stuffed with loud and heavy machinery. And she had a ten-year-old son to look after.

Numb from the loss, hit by the load of responsibility as heavy as the heaps of metal scraps and coal piled up in the yards of her foundries, she went along as if "on autopilot" for a while: her late husband, with his devotion to the business, had run it in such a way that, even when his efforts ceased, the business, this well-oiled machine, carried on moving by inertia. But this would not last forever. The war had ended and life was returning to normality. The machine needed to change route and was rapidly losing momentum. Christina had no choice but to find a way of steering it. Her son John was still far too young to take over, and the only other male family member, Herbert's brother George Northcote, didn't seem to be interested in the business. Actually, we will meet him later in the story, but for now suffice it to say that, after the death of his father and according to the will, George, a young bachelor, had been given a choice of receiving, immediately after tying the knot, either a lump sum of £10,000 or shares in C&H worth £7,000. Not a bad incentive for nuptials! Soon enough he married a girl called Bridget Jones (yes, really!), took the cash and bought a farm in Derbyshire. So – no, he wasn't at all interested in the business. Was his sister-in-law tempted to sell the company and carry on living in relative comfort, raising her child and enjoying the re-established stability in the country slowly recovering from the biggest disaster of the century? Quite possibly – and who would have blamed her?

Instead of quitting, she decided to expand the business. Two managers were hired, one for each foundry: Tom Saw took charge of the Chuckery, and Harry P. Taylor was responsible for Phoenix. Both men knew the trade inside out and were capable of organising the work in the most efficient way. And then, having secured the professional supervision of the production lines, Cristina Bather did what generations of Bathers before her had been reluctant to do: she turned C&H into a public company. This single move, like the proverbial stone, allowed her to solve simultaneously two pressing problems: having sold half of her shares on the Birmingham stock exchange, she raised the capital she needed while still keeping a large stake in the company – and, equally if not more importantly, by ceasing to be the major shareholder, she no longer bore the burden of full responsibility and liability for the enterprise, while still having a say in the decisions taken by the newly created board of directors which she joined.

Here are the members of that very first board of directors of C&H Ltd, now a public company:

G.A.L. Hatton, M.A. (Chairman)
S.H. Hinde, M. Inst B.E., M.I.B.F. (Managing Director)
Mrs C. M. Bather
E.H. Page F.C.I.S. (Secretary)

C&H, like every other company within the industry, faced a difficult task: they had to change from wartime to peacetime production, and they had to do it with a reduced number of skilled workers. This meant significant reorganisation of the production methods. C&H seemed to rise to the challenge: at the first Annual General Meeting, the Chairman stated, *"The Directors feel that we all should be very pleased with the... situation of the Company, as not only have we managed to maintain our tonnage output as compared with the war-time..., but we have also managed to obtain adequate labour at both our foundries, during a period in which most foundries were short of essential production personnel."* However, it became clear that working at maximum capacity during the war had taken its toll on the plant. All the buildings were in need of urgent repairs, and the company's funds were more than sufficient to cover the costs of this patchwork-style overhaul. But the plans of the new management were far more ambitious.

In 1947, C&H received a post-war refund of Excess Profits Tax of £7,301 which could be used only for developing and re-equipping the business. The Government tried to encourage modernisation of the industry by giving companies financial incentives. This could not have happened at a better time: the board had already taken the decision to reconstruct both Walsall and Lichfield foundries, and secured a Development Fund which, together with the money from the Government, allowed the company to undertake a program of substantial renovation. With Christina Bather in charge of the personnel's well-being, an important part of the proposed project was improving the working conditions in the foundries.

To jump-start this program, the company purchased several diesel-driven electricity generators. At the time, blackouts caused by the shortage of coal available to power stations during one of the coldest winters on record were causing serious problems. The generators would make C&H independent of local suppliers in the near future. This was just a prelude to the magnum opus of the impending redevelopment. In 1948, despite the trading profit falling by £597 (the turnover for that period was actually 19% higher than the previous year, but the cost of production had risen sharply; the company absorbed it instead of passing it on to its customers), despite all the problems that came with the reorganisation of labour and the change of product range, a plot of freehold land in Walsall was acquired, and the big project was ready to take off.

14

When size matters
(1951 – 1956)

Chuckery, the company's "first born", hadn't aged well and appeared to be seriously outdated. It had a very low roof making the building dark and dusty, and there was not enough space for any individual moulder to work, if he could and wanted to, at a faster speed than his colleagues on either side of the stall. All this was about to change. In 1951, the old foundry was demolished, and a new, modernised one appeared on the Chuckery's grounds. It included an up-to-date hand moulding section and a pattern shop enhanced with state-of-the-art equipment. The major construction work was completed, according to the chairman's report, *"with the loss of only one day's production… The project would not have been possible but for the loyal cooperation and endeavour of all the employees of the Company."*

The new building offered a far more extensive workplace that not only allowed an increase in the number of moulders by fifty per cent, but also provided each one of them with some additional floor area where he was no longer restricted by the number of moulds he could make before filling them with metal. Now everybody could function at his own pace and within his own space, singlehandedly carrying out all of the operations, from sand preparation through to casting running system knock-off. This method offered several advantages: as every moulder was entirely responsible for the whole process, he was no longer dependent on his co-workers doing their part, so no time was wasted in waiting; and because he could vary the jobs, the levels of fatigue caused by repetition of the same action were significantly reduced. As a result, the production increased by a very tangible 100%. Equally important, even if less tangible and more difficult to measure, was workers' increase in job satisfaction.

By the middle of the twentieth century, the Walsall offices seemed to be worse for wear. Nothing had been spent on them since 1903, so their renovation was long overdue. In 1951, the management approved nearly £2,000 for the improvement of the office block at the Chuckery, and in 1952 the work was completed. From then on, the Annual General Meetings, previously held at the Chamber of Commerce in Tudor House in Walsall, would take place at the newly built premises.

The Chairman summarised the outcomes of the recent redevelopment in his report: "*Walsall Foundry saw changes to buildings that resulted in the doubling of moulding production, and in the five years, reconstruction of the very old offices, a new valve hop with modern plant and gas-fired ovens, a new pattern shop and pattern store, reorganisation of the canteen and welfare amenities with a medical examination room and many other smaller items of improvement.*"

As I remembered, the meetings were held at the Chamber of Commerce, Tudor House, Bridge Street, Walsall. See PDF of the 1949 meeting.

Phoenix, the second C&H foundry, had grown out of its old nest, the disused brewery in Lichfield. The board of directors had even more impressive plans for its redevelopment: an extended foundry was to be constructed behind the existing buildings, allowing free access to the site and causing no interference with production. The old building was to be demolished and replaced by a brand-new frontage filled with a lawn and decorative plants.

The work started in 1952. Christina Bather, widow of Herbert Fiennes and now one of the company's directors, laid the foundation stone of the new foundry. Two Members of Parliament, the Mayor and Sheriff of Lichfield, as well as some major shareholders and all the employees of C&H together with their families were present at the ceremony which took place on the 12th of June. The idea was to accomplish the transition from the old foundry to the new one during the annual holidays at the end of July and the beginning of August to minimise or even avoid any loss of production. And they did it. Within eleven months, the new Phoenix had emerged on the site in accordance with the "guidelines" of the myth (even if not quite from the ashes of the old one), and started production. With the just-fitted modern oil-fired annealing furnaces, it was now capable of delivering a greater amount of castings than ever before.

The final cost of the project was higher than initially thought and came to £110,000 instead of the estimated £87,000. The increase was caused by the higher price of steelwork and electrical installations; also, new production lines were added to the planned ones. But the result was worth the extra spending. In his report, the Chairman described the "reborn" Phoenix as *"one of the best-equipped foundries of its type in the country"*. He added, *"it will provide first-class working conditions"*.

The intense efforts to modernise outdated facilities did not negatively affect the financial resources of C&H, nor did they get in the way of its performance. Here, again, are some lines from the chairman's report: *"during the period in which we have been extensively developing and improving our two foundries, the reserves of your company have been raised from £67,500 on 31st March 1949 to £135,000 on March 31 1954"*. In 1956, the total tonnage produced by Chuckery and Phoenix was more than twice the amount made by the old foundries in 1946, and it continued to increase. The trading profit that year was £95,899 (£2,685,172 today). With room for even more improvement, the company was capable of exceeding that figure. The future looked really bright, and it seemed that the sky was the limit. Except the sky was difficult to see through the thick clouds of smoke when furnaces were in operation.

James William Chamberlin, one of the founding Partners.

Henry Hill, one of the founding Partners

Herbert Fiennes Bather, who was the second Generation of the Bather family involved in the management of Chamberlin & Hill.

Cal Stanley collecting metal ready to pour moulds,
Chuckery foundry circa 1949.

A group photograph of Chuckery Foundry's workforce 1950s.

Christina Millar Bather, the wife of Herbert Fiennes, laying the
foundation stone for the new Lichfield foundry.

The moulding plant producing roller conveyor castings
at Lichfield foundry.

Open day for the visit of dignitaries and customers to view the Walsall foundry's first mechanised plant.

Moulder, Keith Jasper, producing a mould using the snapflask moulding system.

The filling of a ladle from one of the 3-ton electric furnaces at Bloxwich Foundry.

The workforce of the Bloxwich Foundry celebrates the achievement of obtaining the quality standard BS5750.

A caster pouring moulds along the moulding string on Bloxwich Disamatic number two.

The Russel Castings Foundry at Leicester.

Richard Bather, the fourth Generation of the Bather family involved
in management at Chamberlin & Hill.

Barrie Williams, CEO, pictured at the Centenary Dinner along with families, who are descendants of Italian workers at Chuckery works.

A group of Staff members and partners enjoying the evening at the Centenary Dinner.

The workforce following the completion of the
Ductile Castings purchase.

Barrie Williams and the president of Koyama at the Bloxwich foundry.
Viewing the first working digitally controlled grinder outside of Japan.

John Knollys Bather, the third generation, on his retirement day viewing a book on the history of his family's involvement in Chamberlin & Hill.

Jagdev Charna, who was involved in improving production methods of the new lighting systems at Petrel Ltd.

15

Green and other colours of the season, or To Greta with love
(1956 – 1958)

The pollution produced by foundries (all of them, not exclusively those of C&H) seemed to be an inevitable part of the process, sort of a collateral damage, unpleasant but unavoidable: if one wanted to melt metal, one had to heat it by burning coal, if one burnt coal, smoke was produced, if smoke was produced – well, it had to go somewhere… At the time, there were about ten foundries in Walsall, every single one spitting out flames, sparks and fumes from their open top cupolas into the air. The view would have been spectacular – the effects on the atmosphere devastating. The situation in London was even worse: in 1952 alone, severe smog killed more than 4,000 people. Another 8,000 died from related health problems in the months to follow. In the absence of tempestuous Swedish teenagers demanding swift measures against impending doom, the government had to step in. On the 5th of July 1956, The Clean Air Act was published indicating the beginning of the movement towards a cleaner environment. Industries had to respond. The British Cast Iron Research Association came up with the idea of a "wet arrester": a device that could be fitted on top of a foundry's cupola to help stop the spread of dust particles that were thrown into the air. By then, dry (and less effective) arresters had been used by several foundries; C&H, however, pioneered the wet one. Michael M. Hallet, Managing Director, and Tom Shaw, Walsall Works Manager, made a presentation to the Institute of British Foundrymen at their November 1956 meeting, describing the innovation as *"entirely satisfactory in preventing the deposition of troublesome dust on neighbouring dwelling houses and in maintaining a clean roof and guttering of the foundry completely clean."* The system involved recirculation of water which could be also used for quenching when the bottom of the cupola was dropped.

This experiment had proven to be successful enough to attract the attention of the entire industry and, after the Foundry Exhibition later that year, foundries from places as far away from Walsall as Spain approached BCIRA for further information.

As for C&H, they added these arresters to all their cupolas.

If concerns for the environmental issues were universal and actions to address them were required by law, policies regarding the welfare of its employees were instigated and implemented by the company entirely on its own volition. My guess is that to a large extent this was initiated by Christina Bather. Her interest in the working conditions and general well-being of C&H's employees was sincere and not simply imposed on her by her position on the board. She really did her best to keep up the morale of the personnel, from taking into consideration their practical needs (on her initiative, special toilet and shower facilities for Asian workers were installed at the foundries) to organising trips and days out. In June 1958, she hosted a Gala Day for the company's employees, continuing the tradition started years ago by her late husband's father, Herbert Knollys Bather.

On a warm Saturday morning, more than 470 workers and their families arrived at the Wall House in Lichfield, Christina's home. Free coaches were organised to bring people from Walsall and to take them back at the end of the activity-packed day. A twenty-five over cricket match, which had started the festivities, was won by the Lichfield team. I'd like to think that playing on their home territory worked to the advantage of the guys from Phoenix. However, that didn't help them at the tug-of-war competition in which they were beaten by Chuckery. Yes! (I shouldn't really be taking sides, but there you go…) I suppose everybody was a winner in the children-and-mothers' race, as long as all the contestants had fun. Because of the sheer number of people attending, tea had to be served in two sittings in a vast marquee that had been set up in the garden. A fancy dress competition and various performances, including that British classic, a Punch and Judy show, lasted late into the evening.

Overseeing and supervising all of these was Christina's brother-in-law, George Bather. (Remember him? Initially, he chose not to go into the family business and bought a farm with the money he had inherited from his father. After some twenty years of following in the footsteps of an old MacDonald, he realised that it wasn't quite what he wanted and returned to C&H as an administrator at the Lichfield foundry.)

Events like that were just the cherry on the cake and neither the only nor the most significant example of the company's welfare policy. Here is a short extract from the chairman's report in 1957: *"after many discussions with the insurance company, an agreement was reached for the creation of a pension and life assurance scheme… for the benefit of all employees with two years or more of continuous service."* This program came into operation on 1ˢᵗ of April 1957. Next, at an AGM in 1958, the following was announced: *"Separate arrangements suitable for the individual circumstances have been made for those with many years of loyal service who are already too old to be included in any scheme which can be contracted through an insurance company… and we now feel that we have successfully solved the problem of providing the security to which a servant is entitled when he has given loyal and faithful service… for many years."*

These measures brought C&H in line with some of the most progressive companies of the time.

But let us not forget that all the environmental and welfare-related innovations had been happening in parallel with, and as a result of, the company's principal activity, production and trading of iron castings, and by the end of the decade the entire metallurgical industry was facing an increasing number of problems.

16

Vulcan to the rescue
(1959 – 1960)

F or C&H, as for many foundries in the country, 1959 was the most difficult year in more than two decades of trading. The company still made a profit but it was significantly lower than the year before, falling from £79,437 to £47,620. This reduction seemed to have been caused by the intense competition for the decreased volume of demand. Yet, despite the worrying trend, C&H didn't lose a single customer that year. In fact, they even managed to gain a few new ones!

The company adopted a new approach to costing its products. At the time, most foundries calculated the price of a newly introduced casting by comparing it to a similar one already in production. This method didn't take into consideration anything other than the mere likeness of the two.

Chamberlin and Hill Ltd changed this attitude. They wanted to know, with a high degree of accuracy, how much the manufacturing of a new casting would cost and what profit margins should be allowed in order to make a reasonable return. They hired an estimator whose job was to use the drawings of the proposed casting to calculate its weight and to work out the most efficient way of making it. He needed to figure out the optimal number of parts in a mould, weight and production time of the core, inspection time, scrap level, casting metal yield and other steps of the process. Then these variables were used to determine the final price of the product. In April 1958, in anticipation of an imminent recession, it was decided to introduce an up-to-date costing system under the supervision of a professional accountant. The installation was completed by the end of February 1959. This work was carried out by Kenneth Bert Walton, who later would play a much more important role in the running of the company.

Slowly, the demands from nearly all of C&H's customers began to increase, and the Board started to plan for an increase of output instead of looking for additional markets like they had done in the past. As a result, in 1960 they achieved a record turnover. The profit, however, remained the same as two years previously: the margins carried on shrinking due to the rising costs of labour and materials which the company continued to absorb. (According to the chairman's report, that year C&H had done nine per cent more work without receiving any additional income. They had to run faster just to stay in the same place.) This was a problem common to the whole industry, a problem that could have been solved with the help of a new technology. Such technology existed, but not many foundries had actual physical space to accommodate the modern equipment: obtaining plots for extensions next to the existing sites was extremely difficult. Consequently, 370 foundries, almost one in five, had to close down within ten years. All this time, **Chamberlin and Hill Ltd**, acutely aware of the issue, had been purchasing new grounds, wherever they could, more or less continually. In 1961, they bought a small plot adjacent to Phoenix and kept it in reserve for future development. The situation in Walsall was different. It became obvious that, in order to keep up with the demands on the industry, they had to expand the premises. But no room was available next to Chuckery! On three sides the site was surrounded by residential houses and the fourth one was shared with another foundry, **Sydenham and McOustra Ltd**.

The management had to deal with an unpleasant dilemma: to keep the manufacturing process at Chuckery in its technological status quo and be doomed to lose in the escalating competition, or to catch up with the times by introducing a recently developed mechanised plant, capable of boosting the production, in the only area available within the existing site. Unfortunately, that area was far too small to accommodate a plant of the size that would have delivered any noticeable benefits and justified the expense.

Then Vulcan (or Hephaestus if you prefer his Greek counterpart) decided to step in. The mighty god of fire and metalworking must have been in a good mood that day. How else could one explain the fact that just when C&H were struggling to find a solution to their unsolvable dilemma, the foundry adjacent to Chuckery, **Sydenham and McOustra Ltd**, of all possible properties in the country, went up for sale? Norman and Austin Fox, then the directors of **Sydenham and McOustra Ltd**, had decided to retire and offered their next door neighbour, **Chamberlin and Hill Ltd**, to buy the company. The deal was completed on the 18th of August 1960.

Suddenly, the footprint of Chuckery was nearly doubled. Now, instead of squeezing a modestly sized mechanised production line into the premises, they had a perfect chance to modernise the whole site.

17

Business as usual (almost)
(1961 – 1969)

This fortunate acquisition of the neighbouring foundry kick-started an impressive three-stage redevelopment program. To begin with, several outdated buildings were demolished, and the most recent one, erected in 1950, was extended, creating much better working conditions and room for the new mechanised plant. A large hole was knocked through the adjoining wall between Chuckery and ex-**Sydenham & McOustra Ltd**; lintels were put in to support the roof; a monorail, linking the two buildings together, allowed uninterrupted production by supplying molten metal from one cupola to the both sets of moulders. The management retained all the staff of **Sydenham and McOustra Ltd**.

With that, grounds were prepared for the second stage of the programme: the installation of the mechanised plant (known as WM1 or Walsall Mechanised Plant). It was a large oval-shaped flat conveyor, two feet high, with four BMQ3 jolt squeeze machines inside the track making two moulds with core layers working on the outside of the belt. The plant was finally put in place at the end of November 1962 and, after an inevitable adjustment period during which several "teething problems" had to be overcome, it started regular production in March of the following year. It was supervised by John Bather, son of Christina and Herbert Fiennes, who had just joined the company. A young teenager at the time when his mother had had to make life-altering decisions about the fate of the enterprise, now he was twenty-eight years old with experience serving in the British Army behind him.

As well as the introduction of the mechanised production line, the second stage of redevelopment included further extension of the foundry to accommodate new grinding and despatch departments.

All these new additions came at a price. Quite literally. Here are a few lines from Chairman Sir Frederic Scopes: *"Capital expenditure during this year amounted to £111,479, most of which was in respect of the new mechanised plant at Walsall works. This expenditure, together with heavy taxation payments… is responsible for the increase in the bank overdraft from £9,826 to £114,477. I am pleased to say that the overdraft has been reduced steadily since 31*[st] *March 1963."*

Meanwhile, the third phase of the redevelopment was on the way. In July 1964, C&H started negotiations with a neighbouring business, **J.A. Crabtree & Co. Ltd.**, in order to purchase their mechanised foundry plant and transfer it, together with nearly all of its personnel, to Chuckery foundry. The business in question was a company manufacturing electric equipment, and on their premises they had a small foundry which supplied castings for their own principal products. This iron-melting facility, however useful, was nevertheless a bit of a nuisance. It took valuable space and resources, while the castings it provided could have been made elsewhere, and probably more efficiently. C&H volunteered to become this "elsewhere". In July 1964, the deal was struck. By Easter 1965, the plant was incorporated into Chuckery and seamlessly went into production.

To keep up with increased moulding capacity, larger melting units and new cupolas were erected. The effects were felt immediately: in the words of Sir Frederic Scopes, *"the No 1 mechanised plant has, since the beginning of March, been working very efficiently at a level of output not previously obtained."* By the end of 1969, all the benefits of the high levels of capital investment into the Walsall foundry were fully felt.

But that's probably enough about the Chuckery for the moment. What had been happening all this time in Phoenix?

To answer this question, first we would have to specify which Phoenix is meant. The one in Lichfield was doing well after its shell moulding department had been expanded. But now C&H had another facility named after this spontaneously-combustible bird: in October 1967, they purchased a Phoenix foundry and its associated companies in Bloxwich, a small town next to Walsall. It appears that foundries, just like people, had fashions for names, and at the time "Phoenix" was a markedly popular one. But, rather than its linguistic attributes, it was its proximity to Chuckery and the fact that it was specialising in producing malleable iron that attracted C&H's directors to this particular foundry.

However, "Phoenix the second" happened to be less successful than its older namesake. This latest addition to the family of C&H's foundries must have caused its parent company quite a few sleepless nights. Again, let me quote Sir Frederic Scopes: "*I was very disappointed with the results of the Phoenix companies during the year to 30th September 1967. These were, of course, not available to us at the time of completion of the purchase... I am also disappointed that during the six months since 1st October 1967 Phoenix Foundry... did not make any contribution to the profits of the group.*" This failure of the Bloxwich works was caused not only by poor performance but also by the fact that a large stock of castings for conduit fittings, not covered by any order, had been sitting there gathering dust. Both existing directors of the foundry took retirement (and, I can't help wondering, to what extent it was a voluntary decision), and C&H's own John Bather and Harrold Page relocated to Phoenix-2 in order to straighten things up. Helping them was Harry Taylor, who had been the manager of the original Phoenix since 1940 where, in the early fifties, he pioneered the development of shell moulding. The collective wisdom and efforts seemed to be paying off: in 1969, Sir Frederic Scopes noted that "*prospects are better than a year ago... The first trial period of production of grey iron castings was in April and the results are so satisfactory that further periods... have since been run... At present, the prospects for the months ahead are encouraging.*"

Electronic calculator "Anita"

Renovation was coming not only to the actual production lines, but to the office as well. All the calculations for the cost estimates had been handled by comptometer operators specially trained to work with these cumbersome mechanical devices. In the late sixties, the company purchased its very first electronic calculator, named Anita. It was rather unsophisticated, had no memory storage and cost a whopping £480 (£11,468 today). On the plus side, it wasn't very difficult to use. With the foundry production increasing, so was the number of required estimates, and this called for additional devices to help deal with the workload. Rather than buying another calculator like Anita, a decision was made to invest in computerisation of the department. The first computer C&H purchased was an Olivetti Programma 101. The program had to be saved on up to four magnetic cards, and at the end of the calculating process the machine would print a tally roll with the casting price. Sounds a bit primitive? Don't be too quick to judge it: as Gordon, the first person in the company to use this device, found out later, the angle calculations for Apollo's return to Earth after the Moon landing were done on the very same computer! So, if anybody wondered what NASA and C&H have in common...

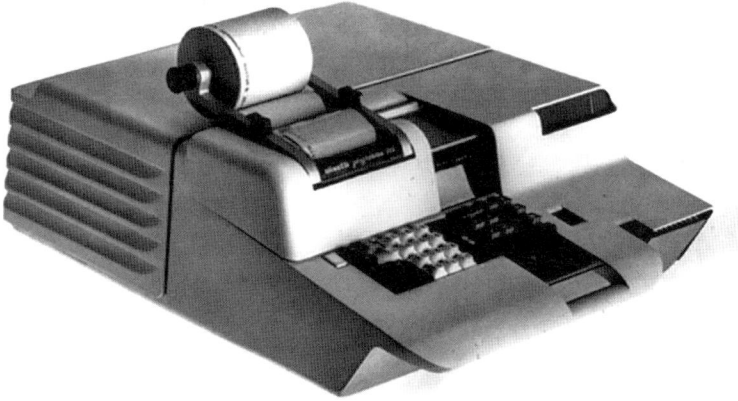

Olivetti Programma 101, first computer purchased by C&H

And, of course, all this site extending, renovating and enhancing was just the background to the manufacturing process taking place. It was business as usual. Or almost...

The profits continued to be good, although they varied from year to year. Here is a small passage from the chairman's report in 1964: "*I am pleased to tell you that the encouraging conditions... were maintained throughout the year with a progressive effect so that each successive quarter has shown an improvement on the preceding one... Relations with customers and suppliers, both equally important, continue to be excellent and we count ourselves fortunate in having this friendly and cordial atmosphere based on mutual trust and confidence.*" The company's representatives were on constant lookout for new orders for both domestic and industrial products. Pictured here is one of these: a meat mincer, manufactured by C&H in the sixties. These handy silver-and-blue devices were really popular in kitchens all over the country because of their unusual design: they attached to the worktop with a suction cup, instead of being clamped to it with a screw which, in time, damaged the surface. Such a simple and brilliant idea wasn't carefully developed on a pristine drawing board by a mechanical engineer with a lab coat and a degree. No, it was Howard Appleby, foreman of the Chuchery's pattern shop and ex-Royal Navy, who sketched his design on the inside of an opened-out cigarette packet during a day visit to Sprong, one of C&H's major customers, a company selling kitchen gadgets, "ancestors" of modern day food processors. Howard proceeded to turn his sketch into a master pattern. Watching him work, amazed by his skill, was young apprentice Gordon Stanley who had just started at **Chamberlin and Hill Ltd** and who, decades later, would be telling me this story. Every year since WM1 had been in operation, C&H manufactured more than 100,000 of these mincers. Would it be possible to estimate the number of burgers and other culinary delights cooked with their help? Among other customers of C&H were **Brook Motors, C&J Hampton, Revvo Casters, Webb Lawnmowers** and **Record Tools**.

Spong Mincer

Here is the Chairman again: *"Though we are by no means a large company by modern industrial standards, you will be interested to know that we are easily amongst the 100 largest iron founders in the country classified by output in tonnes. The Company is large enough to make efficient use of modern plant yet small enough to retain the close personal contacts throughout the organisation."*

These close personal contacts seem to have been a prevalent feature of the company's code of ethics from the very start. The tradition of organising trips and parties for the foundry workers and their families, started by the very first Bather, Herbert Knollys, carried on throughout the passing decades with visits to London and the Lake District. Each Christmas, every employee received a Christmas hamper, choosing from four different types of sets containing cigarettes, luxury food items or bottles of spirits. Later, assembling these parcels became overcomplicated, and they were replaced by vouchers.

In 1963, right in front of the first mechanised plant in Chuckery, golden watches were awarded to the employees who had worked for the company for twenty-five years or more. From then on, this ceremony turned into an annual celebration of loyalty and achievement. Not only did the long-serving members of staff receive meaningful gifts, but also the festive and democratic atmosphere of the events created valuable memories.

Just a year before, in December 1962, the first Open Day took place, another event that was to become a regular feature in the company's social calendar. Initially, prominent figures of the industry and the company's major clients, as well as the mayors of Walsall and Lichfield, were invited to visit Chuckery in order to demonstrate to them its modernised facilities. Sir Cyril Musgrove, chairman of the **Iron and Steel Board,** was heading the party of guests among which were leading officials of the **Joint Iron Council,** the **British Cast Iron Research Association and the Institute of British Foundrymen**, and also representatives of the Ministry of Power. If the aim of the event was to impress the visitors, it worked. Brook Motors, one of C&H's clients, hoping to impress their own customers, produced a booklet about Chuckery's up-to-date facilities.

In 1967, C&H made a tentative step toward stardom in a field far removed from the iron smelting business: Chuckery was attended by Norman Edwards, a cartoonist at the *Birmingham Evening Dispatch* and *Sports Argus,* who was well known for his drawings, caricature-style, of football players and sports personalities. He had decided to visit local companies in search of inspiration and new characters. There was no shortage of those in the Walsall works! (In **"Faces behind the headlines"** below I quote Gordon's description of people featured in the cartoon that appeared in *Birmingham Evening Dispatch* as the result of that encounter.)

Toward the end of the "swinging sixties", arguably the most exciting decade in twentieth century Britain, a decade of intense political and cultural development when the first shoots of growing industrial unrest began to break through the polished but fragile surface of social content, the employees and management of **Chamberlin and Hill Ltd** seemed to be coexisting in a hard-to-achieve harmony. In his report of 1969, Sir Frederic Scopes stressed the *"enthusiastic cooperation"* of all the C&H workers. The situation outside the fences of the company's foundries was, however, not all that congruous: an ever increasing number of spontaneous industrial actions across the country, some unofficial, some supported by unions, heralded troubles to come.

18

Fasten the seatbelts:
turbulence ahead!
(1970 – 1975)

In 1970, Edward Heath was elected as Prime Minister, just as the country was experiencing significant economic decline and social unrest which he tried fixing by attempting to weaken the power of the unions. It didn't fare well. Unions fought back using the most potent weapon in their arsenal: organised general strikes. The economy took hit after hit like a punch bag in a boxing gym.

To start with, **Chamberlin and Hill Ltd** seemed to be largely unaffected by this violent clash of giants, at least according to its chairman Sir Frederic Scopes: in his statement at the end of 1970 there is very little reference to the outside influences on the company. In fact, he even praised "*improved communications and the encouragement of genuine team spirit throughout the organisation*". Life had to go on, and important business-related decisions continued to be taken. A piecework payment system was adopted by different departments. This scheme allowed the estimators to accurately judge the wages for core-making, moulding, grinding and all the ancillary operations. Tom Martin, a management consultant and a board member of **P.A. Management Consultants** who had put this system in place, became deputy chairman of C&H. The news concerning the Bloxwich foundry was particularly reassuring: the previously failing Phoenix-2 and its associated companies, having undergone some changes to its managerial structure, finally began to make a considerable contribution to the company's profits. Quoting the report, "*Indeed, the* *improvement during the second half of the year was due entirely to Bloxwich."* This trend would continue into the near future.

The tensions between the government and unions continued to escalate, and C&H could not escape their impact for long. In 1971, Tom Martin, now the Chairman, reported: *"The immediate prospects for the current year are not as bright as they were this time last year. The rate of order inflow, in common with that of the industry, began to fall during December 1970 and at present shows very little sign of improvement."* Indeed, it would have been blatantly unrealistic to have a more optimistic prognosis in a country about to plunge into the Dark Ages. I mean this quite literally: in 1972, for the first time since 1926, miners stopped working over a pay rise dispute. At the time, most electricity in the UK came from coal, so no coal meant serious blackouts. The working week was limited to three days. Candlelit dinners did not mean romance but became the only alternative for consuming food in the dark. In Downing Street, even meetings of the Cabinet were illuminated by candles.

Under the circumstances, it's hardly surprising that the profits of the company dropped. What might be considered surprising is the fact that, despite the extremely difficult trading conditions, C&H not only managed to still make a profit, however reduced, but also continued to expand. The renovation of the Walsall foundry had just entered its final stage. By September 1972, a new dispatch bay with a warehouse and two mechanised production lines were completed, and the new office block was added to the existing one, creating a modern and spacious head office. A number of improvements on a smaller scale happened to both the Lichfield and Bloxwich foundries as well.

On the first of January 1973, twelve years after first applying for membership, Great Britain finally joined the EEC, the European Economic Community. C&H didn't wait long to use the opportunities this offered. Their Chairman, Tom Martin, led a Trade Mission to France, organised by **Birmingham Chamber of Commerce**. That year, the company's direct exports doubled and included sales to the USA, New Zealand, Belgium and Sweden. After the regression in 1972, things were beginning to look up.

Then, on the 9th February 1974, the miners whose demands of a seven per cent wage increase had not been met, came out on strike again. Aware of the shaky economic situation in the country in the wake of the

Arab Israeli conflict and the substantial oil price hike that followed, unions were determined to use it to their advantage. The Government refused to cave in. Prime Minister Edward Heath declared a State of Emergency and a three-day working week. The effects of such measures were immediately felt by the industry. Tom Martin announced in his annual report: "*The problems associated with the fuel crisis and the period of three days working seriously affected the profitability.*" Even more disturbingly, C&H "*was not immune from the labour disputes… The situation was made more difficult by a chronic shortage of suitable labour and… the foundries are currently operating 10% below strength.*" These labour disputes had been caused by substandard working conditions at Phoenix Bloxwich, the least modern of the three foundries belonging to C&H, and would result in management's decision to intensify improvements in that area. Adding insult to injury was an unprecedented rate of inflation: the cost of scrap and pig iron increased by sixty per cent, and most of the other materials and services vital for a foundry's operation also went up in price. By law, all the companies were required to absorb approximately fifty per cent of all wage and salary awards which would further shrink profit margins. These highly unfavourable conditions not only held the company back in the meantime, but also caused management's concerns for the future: such restrictions were threatening the accumulation of reserves necessary for capital and technology investment which had marked C&H out since its very foundation.

During this truly catastrophic year, the company still managed to generate a profit of £235,000 (£2,504,645 today) on a turnover of £2.8 million (£29,842,580). How was it possible, when all the factors influencing the commercial success of a business, seemed to conspire against it? This rhetorical, at first glance, question, actually has an answer. It was partially given by Tom Martin in his report: "*Company has always recognised the need to keep abreast of technical developments and to improve environmental conditions, both internally and externally.*" Such a policy, despite the high implementation costs involved, "crisis-proofs" a business and guarantees significant steady returns on the investments in the long term, regardless of the economic conditions. And yet again, they had been right: compared to 1974, profits in the following year nearly doubled at £463,000 (£3,971,908). Intelligent planning and strategic investments of the past were paying off in the present. Now it was time to secure equally satisfactory results in the future.

At the end of January 1975, C&H purchased the whole of the share capital of **Conduit Fittings Ltd**. A long-established Walsall company manufacturing a range of conduit fittings based on malleable iron castings, it represented an allied trade and was situated close to the existing sites of C&H, allowing it to diversify its business interests.

Supplements to Part III
Faces behind the headlines

In 1967, *Birmingham Evening Dispatch* published Norman Edward's cartoon after his visit to Chuckery. Here is what Gordon Stanley remembers about people who had inspired the drawing:

> George Stanton, *as the cartoon states, was always known as Jackie Stanton. He oversaw the inspection shop and knew every casting by its part number. Jackie, who stood less than five feet tall, was a very lively, always happy character. He kept the inspection shop busy, which, in turn, pressurised the grinding shop to keep the throughput into the despatch.*

> Fred Wilkinson *was an ex-Sydenham and McOustra member of staff, a brilliant artist. His pictures, including the one of Lichfield cathedral, drawn in fine detail, hung in several offices.*

> John Stanley, *also known as Jack, is shown in the cartoon as a fisherman, but his real joy was ballroom dancing. In his younger days, he was part of a formation dance team winning many trophies.*

> Edith Fletcher, *Edie, was second in charge in the canteen, but you wouldn't have known that. She was never one to stand on ceremony but worked hard to supply the workers with two meals a day and a snack in the afternoon.*

> Richard Holland, *or Dick, was an ex-snap flask moulder, at the time of Norman's visit in charge of the WMI plant. He was very conscientious about his job. The workers of a similar age always pulled his leg about wearing a hair net when he played football, which he never denied.*

Frederick Burns, *as the cartoon says, was always known as Tubby, but didn't appear to carry any excess weight. When collecting his 25 years' service Gold Watch he appeared in his working clothes, which left John Bather feeling embarrassed. He said: "Tubby, you scruffy bugger, you could have changed into a suit!" Tubby replied: "I earned it in my dirt, I'll collect it in my dirt." Sir Frederic Scopes, who was handing out the awards, said: "Quite right, Tubby!" – and shook his hand as enthusiastically as all the other workers.*

Sidney Bentley, *at the time a grinder who would later take over the foremanship of the broaching shop. By then that department would have expanded with many women doing numerous jobs like drilling, broaching, painting and bagging ready for despatch, so Sid was kept on his toes.*

Annie Bray, *a woman of small stature one hundred percent dedicated to her work. Just before her retirement she was awarded a British Empire Medal for services to the industry which was well deserved.*

Abdul Karim, *in charge of the cupolas, a very responsible job, learnt his trade from Jack Steppard. Abdul was one of the first Indian workers at C&H and a leader of his community.*

Levi Pascall, *as the cartoon suggests, would be working during the holiday re-bricking the Cupola. The area opposite the charge door had the most wear and would need taking back to the steel outer tube before the new refractory bricks were put in place with the gannister lining on top and slowly cured before re-lightning in the small hours on the day the foundry returns from the break.*

Joe Scott *was a chief inspector who had started at Chamberlin and Hill in 1965. Ex-Royal Marine and ex-patternmaker, he did not take a step back from anybody. Over the years he saved C&H a small fortune. When a problem occurred, the first reaction from most customers was to blame the casting – so Joe would visit them and in the vast majority of cases be able to point out the real cause.*

Howard Dunn, *known as Lofty to his colleagues, was a shot blaster, cleaning the sand off the castings before they went to the inspection. He worked alongside Charlie Day, another long-time employee of the company. The castings would be fed to the shot blaster in metal pans holding between 25 and 40 kilograms. They had to swing this pan into the waist-high rotating drum, taking three to four pans to fill it: hard work for guys reaching 60. Howard's wife Emma also worked for C&H being in charge of the hand-made core department.*

Founder's
Sorcerer's apprentice

For a young guy, fresh out of school, the way into the heavy metal industry would have been through an apprenticeship. This is how Gordon Stanley started his work at Chamberlin and Hill, and this is what it was like for him and, I guess, for many more budding founders. (Except for the romantic consequences of his apprenticeship: that was not necessarily included in the curriculum…)

"In June 1962, I started at Chamberlin and Hill, Chuckery, Walsall, where my family worked. I waited for a few months for an opening in the Pattern shop as an Apprentice Patternmaker.

When you arrived each day at C&H, you were required to clock in. A machine would stamp your card with the time when you pushed the handle down. Tom Beard, the company's security and first aid officer, was always present to prevent anyone from clocking other employees' cards. Tom would have to write the time on your card if the clock didn't work or punch correctly.

Work would start at eight o'clock. You had to make all the senior patternmakers a cup of tea and carry on with that throughout the day. Life at that time seemed to consist of tea making, cup washing, sweeping the shop and any other menial task that the senior patternmakers asked you to do. Luckily, another apprentice shared the burden, so we did weeks about giving us time to learn some patternmaking skills.

My first job at the factory was to work in the machine shop, drilling and tapping cast parts for assembly working alongside Charlie Padmore, Philip Frankham, Elsie Bond, and her sister Ethel Glynn. There was already one apprentice there, John Russell, and two other fully qualified patternmakers who had started their part-time businesses: Terry Braide who had a mobile fish and chip shop, and Trevor Butler, owner of a mobile greengrocery. The firm thought that all three were not fully committed, and I was to go into the pattern shop once these guys had worked their notice, which, in those days, was only one week. I thought this should be a very secure position as every pattern used in the foundry was made on site.

An apprentice at that time was required to work a forty-two-hour week. Out of this, you were allowed one day off to go to Wednesbury Technical College, studying Engineering, the basics of machining, drilling, using a turning lathe with cutting depths and drill speeds and learning how to sharpen drills and the tools of the trade, but you also had to give up two nights for two three-hour evening sessions out of your own time. All for the princely sum of two pounds, seven shillings and sixpence a week (£2.37 in today's money): this was the union rate for a sixteen-year-old apprentice. The only concession given to an apprentice was a reduced cost of lunch in the works canteen. Workers over eighteen years of age paid a shilling (5 pence), but we paid only sixpence (2 1/2 pence). There was a full range of meals with bacon or sausage sandwiches or toast at breakfast. At lunchtime, there would be the choice of meals with a roast on most days and then bread pudding for the afternoon break. Running the kitchen was Mrs Brown, helped by Edith Fletcher.

We had a lot to learn, so we came under the supervision of the senior patternmakers, the best in their respective fields: Jack Newton would show us all facets of Milling machines, George Appleby introduced us to moulding and making double-sided plates, Dennis Beard taught us lathe turning and broach making, Alf Golder – oddsides, and Alf Gudgin was the guy from whom I learned a lot about moulding. Alf worked past his retirement age, looking after the melting of metal for the pattern shop. He was a man of vast experience in individual moulding, always ready to help if you had difficulty moulding or pouring a casting. Alf would tell of the working regime in the foundry at the turn of the century when he was a fourteen year old lad. Then, he was employed by the moulder, not the foundry owner. He would be at the foundry at 5 a.m. to light the small open-hearth furnace and get the metal melted in a crucible in time for the moulder to start. He remembered how once, when he had been late getting up and failed to get the metal ready for his boss, the moulder: "I got a good backhander and was told that next time I would be out of work!" And I thought that we had a hard life...

By 1963 and for the following two years, the two days that we were going to technical College were Wednesday (6.30 p.m. till 9.30 p.m.) and Friday (9.00 a.m. till 9.30 p.m.) Friday was the worst night as far as any young man was concerned, because you could not collect your wages, which were paid in cash at four o'clock that day, and had to wait until Monday unless Jess Orbell, the wages clerk, worked on Saturday morning. On Friday nights, we were working while all our friends were out on the town having fun. After technical College, we had to catch the bus home. At that time, pubs had a calling time of ten o'clock, so if you wanted that pint, you really had to rush!

After a year at the college, I had to spend a month at the National Foundry Craft Training Centre, at Swan Lane, West Bromwich, and board at their in-house facility for apprentices from all over the country.

It was during this period, as an apprentice, we were required to carry heavy parcels, mainly customers' sample castings, to help the office junior, Linda, take them to the local post office at the end of Beacon Street, after talking a few times, asked her for a date and the rest is history.

Following the introduction of the Foundry Industry Training board during Harold Wilson's Labour government, the firm could claim back part or all of a levy placed on companies by offering better training to everyone. As a result, apprentice training was expanded. You had to spend six months in each department. My first stint was moulding in the foundry under an experienced moulder named Bernard Harrison, the father of the other patternmaking apprentice, Colin. Bernard would receive the casting requirements from George Miller, the production manager, and decide how to split up the work between himself, 'Bowie' Yates, his work colleague and me. By then, I had learned a lot from Alf Gudgin, so the moulding part posed no difficulty. What was new to me was carrying a shank of metal, around 60lbs (27 kg) in weight at 1500C, running approximately forty yards to the mould, but it's the type of thing that you just got on with the job.

I also spent time in the core shop; women carried out most of the core making. Names that come to mind are Emma Dunn, whose husband Howard (Lofty) operated the shot-blast machines and later worked in the despatch. There was also Nellie Porter, Jeanne McDonald, and Betty Millard, who ran the Polygram machine, a new introduction at the same time as WM1. This machine could make sixteen shell cores simultaneously, mainly mincer cores, to form the internal shape through which the meat was forced. Traditionally, cores were a mixture of sand and molasses, which was hand rammed into aluminium core boxes then turned out onto core shells to go into the core oven to be cured.

I then had to go off-site to spend six months on a job swap with an apprentice in a master pattern shop called Crockett Lowe Ltd., a firm with a big reputation in the Patternmaking industry.

One day in 1966, Mr John Bather called us to his office with Stan Weaver, the Training Manager. He said that he would like us to go on an Outward-Bound Course. Very few dates were available, so we ended up on Dartmoor at Holne Park for four weeks, starting on 30th January. Winters then were a little worse than they are now. Approximately half of the time we spent under canvas on Dartmoor on snow-covered ground: thick clothes and a strong constitution were necessary. Rock climbing, abseiling, caving, canoeing, and rope climbing were offered as part of an assault course. I led the climb. Each morning following a ten-minute run, we took a dip in the River Dart, which in February was cold. You then had a ten-minute run back to the house for a precise one minute under a hot shower. The idea was to challenge you and put you outside your comfort zone, and I think I had met every challenge.

To expand our knowledge of the foundry, we were tasked to work in parts of the foundry for six months periods, in the Core making, Moulding, and Estimating. At the end of this period in the Estimating, I was offered a position on the staff as an Estimator working for Mick Smith. A staff position guaranteed you an annual salary and a pension that you paid a contribution towards.

Coming up was our advanced City and Guilds exam in Foundry Technology and Patternmaking. My father thought it would be great for me to get a Distinction, which meant receiving an 80% mark. No C&H apprentice had ever achieved this. Our results came back in the middle of August. Worried that I had not done well enough,

I didn't race home that evening. A brown envelope marked City & Guilds was placed upright against the clock on the mantelpiece. I had to face the inevitable. I opened the envelope: the first sheet stated that I got a Credit in Patternmaking with 79%. I'd missed the distinction by one. Expecting a worse result in Foundry Technology, the more complex subject, I pulled out the second card, and to my surprise and Dad's, the word Distinction was prominent.

The next day the company had also received our results, and Stan Weaver asked me to accompany him up to the Managing Director's office. Mr Halett congratulated me on the work and said it was the best result for all apprentices, past or present. I was given the option of continuing studies or remaining as a staff member, and chose the latter."

HISTORY OF
CHAMBERLIN AND HILL

PART

4

19

From West Midlands to Midwest (and some other places)
(1976 – 1978)

A respectably large dark blue Vauxhall was slowly reversing into a free bay right outside the office building of **Aldridge Bells**, car dealers in the north of Birmingham. Scarce rays of wintry sun, bouncing off the polished bonnet, looked like the festive illumination of Christmas just gone. The garage manager, whose name did not get recorded in the annals of history, was watching the vehicle through his office window with interest. *Maybe my luck is about to change,* thought he (the business had been incredibly sluggish recently). The Vauxhall finally stopped, its front doors flew wide open and two men stepped out of the saloon onto the wet tarmac. *Or maybe not,* concluded the manager. An inexplicable contrast between the sleek appearance of the executive car and that of the outlandish visitors now standing next to it did not promise a successful deal. The passenger, a short and stocky guy, seemed to have been avoiding hairdressers for the best part of the year. The driver, tall and straight, wore a shabby overcoat which must have been used as an oversized oven glove or fire blanket: it had burn marks all over. Supplementing his outfit was a trilby hat with a matching hole right at the front. One of the sales staff, a young inexperienced lad, approached the extravagant pair. The manager saw the oven-glove-wearer saying something, opening the car door, dipping inside and emerging with a logbook which he then handed to the sales boy.

It was time to intervene. The manager rushed outside. The lad was already by the door. *"They want to sell it. And they want cash."* he said, giving the log book to the manager who, having quickly leafed through it, replied: *"Run to my office, grab the Yellow Pages and find the number of..."* – he studied the page with the name of the registered vehicle owner – *"... Chamberlin and Hill. Tell them that these two gypsy characters are trying to sell us their car. Then phone the police."* With that, he carried on towards the clients: *"How can I help you... gentlemen?"*

Two minutes later the lad came out of the office with an expression of disbelief on his face: *"It's okay Sir. I got to speak with Mr Walton there. He said, they are their Managing Director and their works engineer..."*

The man wearing a fire-bitten coat was, indeed, John Bather, now the Managing Director of the company that he had joined nineteen years ago and that had been run so successfully by his father and grandfather before him. Did he inherit their exceptional leadership skills?

Well, not quite. I am under the impression that he really did try. "Eccentric to the last degree", as described by some people I talked to, he walked around foundries for twenty years wearing the same coat (which made sense: why change if you spend a lot of your time next to the flame-spitting furnaces?), knew most workers by their first names and offered solutions to daily problems, like finding a way of getting a better price for the company car that was no longer needed. But he was not a Hannibal of the corporal world. Managing a large company requires strategic thinking, and not everyone is a born strategist. Luckily, John Bather didn't need to be one. He was assisted by his "talented lieutenants", experts in their fields: Ken Walton, the Group Finance Director, who was responsible for the profitable acquisition of suitable businesses allowing **Chamberlin and Hill Ltd** to grow, and Barry Williams, Group Production Director, a qualified metallurgist with the ability to achieve maximum improvement of the production methods with minimal investment. It has to be said that, from the very start, C&H has had the privilege of employing some of the most capable and enthusiastic people in the industry. The list of all who had been in charge of the company will follow at the end of the book, but for now let us return to the mid-seventies and the challenges that came with the time.

Inflation was spiralling out of control. Today, as I am writing this, the inflation rate has reached 10%, causing understandable worry and concerns within society. In 1975, it was 24.11%. Financial markets no longer had confidence in sterling. To avoid a total crash, in 1976 the

Labour Government was forced to turn to the **International Monetary Fund** to be bailed out. The IMF imposed its terms, one of which was the reduction of public spending. Order books of the UK's companies were shrinking. The choice for most was to either lose customers or absorb the increase of production costs. One way or the other, the profits were to suffer. So was 1977 going to be the first year in its long history that C&H would trade at a loss?

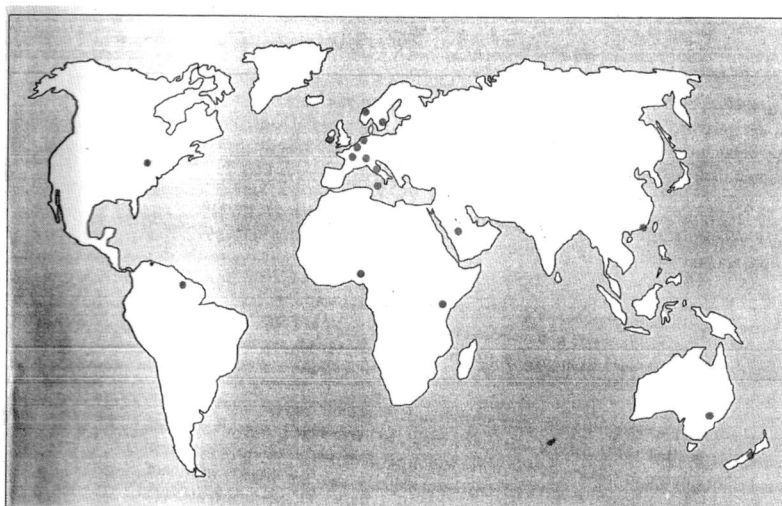

America
Australia
Belgium
France
Guyana
Hong Kong
Ireland
Italy
Kenya
Malta
Middle East
Netherlands
New Zealand
Nigeria
Norway
Sweden
Switzerland

Check out this little map

It did look that way, at least to start with. Even if its own subsidiary company, **Conduit Fittings Ltd**, enabled Bloxwich foundry to maintain the full production capacity, the other two, the Walsall and Lichfield works, functioned only part-time. But within a problem often lies its solution. The state of the UK's economy was reflected in the exchange rate of the pound, creating perfect conditions for export sales. C&H seized this opportunity. Harrold Page, who was about to retire in April, accepted an invitation to stay on the Board as Export Director for two more years. He travelled the world, singlehandedly arranging deals that would prove to be very successful. The Chairman explained in his report: *"Because of lack of confidence in the UK economy, Your Company has devoted a lot of energy to its exporting activity and… I am happy to report a further significant increase in our overseas business."*

C&H went global. Antarctica was the odd one out because C&H did not sell any of their products there, but on every other continent they did. Check out this little map decorated with dots indicating the presence of C&H in those regions: from Norway to New Zealand, from the American Midwest to the Middle East – the list of destinations to which a couple of small towns in the West Midlands sent boxes of heavy cargo is impressive. What exactly did their overseas customers want to buy? That varied. **Geerpres Inc** from the USA commissioned bucketfuls of mop presses, mechanisms that, despite looking like torture devices, were most benign in nature and, being fixed on top of a bucket, squeezed excess water from a mop, making floor cleaning a bit easier. For **Curt Bjorkner**, Sweden, C&H manufactured hand clamps. Dutch company **Prins Metallurgische** bought joints for connecting Dividag reinforcement bars. Those were then cast into concrete blocks used to build suspension bridges. An Italian firm **Salvatore Palliatoe** ordered grips for clamping wire ropes that could be found in various devices, from lifts to exercise machines.

Such transactions were booming: in 1977, the very year when absence of profit seemed unavoidable, the value of the exported goods reached £557,444 (£2.645 million today). Domestic sales were more modest but still profitable, with the largest contribution of £69,294 (£328,771) coming from the newest part of the group, **Conduit Fittings Ltd**. Yet again the policy of expanding the business and investing into new technologies was paying off. While a great number of British investors were losing money, the shareholders of C&H received the maximum permitted dividend. So the decision to spend £175,000 in order to buy two more companies located in Walsall, **Platt Malleable Castings Ltd.** and **Arthur Morgan (Engineers) Ltd.**, made perfect sense. The second was needed to complement the electrical fittings activity. The existing parts of the business continued to be upgraded: a second Hallsworth plant (WM4) was commissioned for Chuckery.

By 1979, Harrold Page's peregrinations had come to an end with him finally taking that long-overdue retirement. The stream of international orders started to fade away, and C&H could no longer rely on the income they generated. To remain profitable, the company had to concentrate its efforts on the domestic market.

20

On challenges of being
an Evergreen
(1979 – 1989)

The volatile economic situation in the country reflected the general state of society. Plenty has been written about that period; I don't need to repeat here what a great number of scholars, journalists and fiction writers have already said, but in a nutshell: right in the middle of the extremely cold winter of 1978 to 1979, the third coldest in the twentieth century, thousands of strikes shook Britain, sending shock waves into the future, ripping through the fabric of the economy and affecting every business in the country. And, just like in the real snowy landscape where most plants go dormant or even die while only evergreens stay strong and flourish, in the metaphorical landscape of the "winter of discontent" a lot of British companies had no choice but to scale down their activity. Some of them disappeared altogether, yet others seemed to be thriving in spite of the adverse conditions. **Chamberlin and Hill Ltd** belonged to the latter category. What did it take, what allowed them to become such an "evergreen" of the business world?

At first glance, the solution was obvious: prepare to be flexible and react to the fluctuations of the market as soon as they happen. Or, better still, even before. Something like what C&H seems to have been doing that decade.

The main feature of the company's policy at the time was the diversification of its business. Having "dipped a toe in the water" in 1975 by purchasing **Conduit Fittings Ltd**, a firm specialising in, as the name suggested, production of conduit fittings used for making connections in a variety of electric systems, C&H began venturing out into a wider area of the market. Owning an engineering business guaranteed them more room for manoeuvre on this new territory. The project met the expectations. To reinforce the latest development, another engineering firm, **Solenoids and Regulators Ltd**, was purchased in 1979 which, in the words of Chairman John Robert Eades, *"has considerably strengthened our position in the flameproof switchgear market… The benefits of diversification… are already apparent, and the Directors are confident that the greater spread of markets now available to the group will prove to be of inestimable value in the future."*

He was right: in the next couple of years, **Solenoids and Regulators Ltd**, even if functioning below predicted productivity some of the time, still outperformed the foundries. This wasn't a fluke: while the foundry industry continued to feel the effects of the miners' strikes, the housing market was beginning to grow which greatly increased the need for electrical installations. C&H were suppliers of components to engineering companies whose major customer, the **National Coal Board**, had to significantly cut down its orders. The overcapacity within the sector forced some of the foundries to drop their prices to unsustainable levels, but C&H didn't plan to choose that route which, eventually, would lead to a dead end. Keeping costs realistic enabled them to securely maintain the quality of their products throughout – although in the short term this meant losing a number of customers to competitors concerned predominantly with immediate gains. From the chairman's report in 1982: *"In my opinion, it is better to batten down the hatchets and ride the storm on the theory that a moribund market cannot be revived… by price-cutting."* Costs of ferrous scrap and coke were rising sharply. And, to make problems more complex, consumer behaviour was changing in tune with the time. As more and more people were discovering the joys of ready-made meals, their interest in traditional cookware was fading. Who wants to struggle handling a cast iron casserole dish, as heavy as a set of dumb bells, if one could stick a sleek container with some food proxy into a microwave oven and save time and effort while feeling hip and modern? Seduced by the promise of a hassle-free future of housekeeping, housewives strolled indifferently past the supermarket shelves loaded with old-fashioned kitchen implements.

The engineering companies had been purchased just in time to keep the whole group afloat. But the demand for their products was shifting:

orders for switchgear and standard conduit fittings increased significantly while selling equipment like flameproof junction boxes to the processing companies was no longer a viable option because of the cut-backs in the petro-chemical industry. In response to these changes, the board took a decision to reorganise the constituents within the group. On the 1st of April 1982, a new company was created. Named **Petrel Ltd**, it absorbed **Solenoids and Regulators Ltd** and the range of flameproof appliances formerly produced by **Conduit Fittings Ltd.**

Both **Conduit Fittings**, now devoid of its flameproof range, and the newly established **Petrel**, continued to outperform the iron smelting part of the group. After a very short-lived improvement at the beginning of 1982, the demand for castings plummeted again. Keeping all the C&H's plants became unsustainable. O'Henry's *"Bolivar cannot carry double"* springs to mind... Something had to go. **Leamore Lane foundry** (previously **Platt Malleable**) ceased production in February 1982, only five years after being purchased. The decision to close it can't have been easy but it made sense. The real blow came later when, in 1985, it became apparent that even without the Leamore Lane foundry, Bolivar was still struggling.

At the time, the Lichfield plant, namesake of the mythical bird, was failing. Working only three days a week, Phoenix was losing customers attracted by reduced prices elsewhere. In 1983, the management of sales at C&H was decentralised, and Phoenix received its own commercial department based at the foundry. It was run by Gordon Stanley. By then, my guide through the world of molten metal had worked at the company for twenty-two years, rising in ranks from an apprentice. Having graduated from college with a distinction, he was given the choice of continuing his education or remaining a member of staff at C&H, and he chose the latter. He worked at the estimating department covering estimates for Bloxwich Foundry; in 1978 he was promoted to Assistant Commercial Manager, and five years later became Sales Executive at Lichfield. His mission was to revive the foundry's formerly full order book. Which he did.

Only doing it had not been as straightforward as it was for me to write that phrase. It turned out to be a real adventure, a combination of extensive travel, negotiations and even re-designing and re-inventing certain products. Here are some examples: in order to get back **Fenner Mech.** and **Fletcher Sutcliffe Wild**, two old customers who had started using another foundry's castings in their milling machines on request of the **British Coal Board**,

Gordon, realising that the competitor was not able to maintain their unjustifiably low prices, painstakingly visited every manufacturer involved, demonstrating to them the advantages of realistic pricing. Increasing the number of orders from an American company based in Bradford, **Schwitzer Turbochargers**, required providing a prototype of a modified design that resulted in lowering production costs. (Oh, this one came with an added benefit of picking up a new client, **Garret Air Research**, in the process.) To get more work from **Concentric Pumps**, Gordon needed to hand modify a core for a casting of an oil pump and make a sample. The new design was approved; the production of that particular part remained with C&H for years to come. This list can be continued. As a result of Gordon's efforts, Lichfield's order book in 1983/84 was full, the foundry returned to a five-day week, and Phoenix began to make profit again. To a large extent this was due to regaining the contract with the **NCB**.

The miners' strike of 1984 undercut all the hard work. Without the orders for the conveyor roller – and **NCB**, understandably, had to dramatically reduce those – Lichfield foundry was thrown back to being a non-profitable part of the group, quickly turning into a ballast too heavy to carry along. From the chairman's report in 1986: "*In December last year we decided with regret that the market for grey iron castings would no longer support two foundries. We therefore announced the closure of our Lichfield factory… In the changed market conditions, we have therefore consolidated production in the Walsall foundry.*" After nearly a hundred years of service, Phoenix failed to regenerate.

The process of selling the site took a year and, continuing the analogy with Greek mythology, turned into a battle of Titans. There were three of them, **Chamberlin and Hill Ltd, Safeway Supermarkets** (a potential buyer) and **Lichfield City Council**. In January 1987, both Safeway and Tesco, another commercial giant, submitted a planning application involving a site near Phoenix. Lichfield District authorities decided that the city didn't need two large supermarkets next to each other, partially because this would have drawn the public away from the city centre, and declined Safeway's proposal, which automatically devalued by half the land still owned by **Chamberlin and Hill Ltd**. The company initiated a public enquiry. The procedure was likely to drag along for some time – until the legal counsel employed by C&H came up with a universally satisfying solution: they proposed using part of the development as a "park and ride" area, encouraging shoppers to go to the city centre while automatically reducing traffic and pollution in that area. Lichfield council's opposition to the scheme had been overthrown by the decision of a government inspector, and the deal was completed, bringing C&H an extraordinary £1,118,000. Phoenix might have failed to re-generate, but it had still managed to generate a great profit.

The challenging trading conditions and loss of one of the oldest parts of the group highlighted the need to re-think the way the company was organised and run. Previously managed from the centre, in 1986 it was broken down into three distinct sectors: grey iron, malleable, and engineering divisions under the directorship of Barrie Williams, Ken Walton and Alf Edwards respectively. Each division had its own dedicated sales and estimates department. Gordon Stanley left Lichfield to take over the Commercial Management, Sales and Marketing department of the Malleable Division. The Chairman explained the idea behind the new development: "*This… has enabled us to concentrate production on four sites where previously we operated on seven. This rationalisation has been accompanied by continuing modernisation of the facilities at both our remaining foundries and at our two electrical equipment works…*"

The most significant advancements were happening in Bloxwich. After well over twenty years of almost no investments, now it was having a full make-over. In 1983, it received a new Disamatic moulding plant which allowed workers to place twenty cores into the moulds within the standard time. And just a few years later, on the 13th of November 1986, the first Radyne three-tonne medium frequency electric furnace was installed there with two more to follow shortly. This presented exciting opportunities like expanding the range of materials produced, which, in turn, would lead to C&H entering new markets. (In fact, sixteen per cent of all orders received by the foundry since then were orders for spheroidal graphite iron, a substance known for its higher tensile strength and elongation but requiring specific melting conditions that had been impossible to achieve in the traditional furnace.) It also improved the environment for both the foundry's workers and its neighbours. Non-dependence on the availability of coal at the time of miners' strikes would have been an added bonus: until then, they had been keeping adequate amounts of coke by sending lorries all the way to Belgium and stockpiling it at the Lichfield site, but, without Phoenix, storage would have become more problematic.

As expected, the "new and improved" Bloxwich foundry had attracted "new and diverse" customers, while retaining the existing ones despite the long-overdue increase in prices. An explosion of designs followed. Here is a small selection of what was produced at Bloxwich after the introduction of the smart equipment: most parts of cast conveyor chains for **Edward Chain**; anti-sway devices and security fixtures for caravans and homes on request from **Bulldog Security Products**; quick connectors for the slip lock scaffolding systems ordered by **S.G.B. Scaffolding**; connectors for gas piping for industrial as well as domestic use required by **Georg Fisher**. Valve guards were specifically designed and made for air pumps: to prove their safety, these had to pass a strict testing regime and were to remain undamaged and fully operational after being dropped from a height of two metres onto a steel base. Kee Klamps coupler castings produced by Bloxwich were intended to join any kind of tubing and had too many applications to list here. But I will still mention one: which can be found – probably even now – in the USA early warning system in Alaska, as part of radars apprehending Russian Missiles. But the essential part of C&H's order book consisted of the requests from the railway companies such as **Balfour Beatty Rail Engineering**, **Recife Light Railway** and **Hong Kong LTR**. For those, Bloxwich foundry manufactured castings for polymeric insulators used in both overhead power distribution to the national grid and overhead electrification of railway infrastructure.

Maintaining close relationships with all the companies within that sector was the responsibility of Richard Bather, the fourth generation Bather family member who had only recently joined the firm.

The results were not immediate – but no-one expected them to be. From the chairman's report: *"Whilst we have made progress over this period of change, profits paused in 1985-86 with trading profit before tax and profit after tax both being down from £562,000 to £531,000 and from £339,000 to £319,000 respectively."* By contrast, here is what the same chairman stated only two years later: *"The year under review (1988) was one of all round progress for Chamberlin and Hill. The profit before tax was… £1,229,000. After charging tax of £393,000 the profit was £836,000… Total sales rose by 12% and margins widened to 9.4%. All the manufacturing units made a healthy contribution toward the achievement…"*

Acknowledging the fact that it was the engineering companies that helped the group to remain profitable in the times when foundries struggled to stay afloat, and having returned to its habitual high-profit existence, C&H quite predictably continued to expand by buying more potentially beneficial businesses. 1989 was the year of acquisitions: two more companies joined the group.

The first one was a local firm, **Fred Duncombe** of Cannock. The largest manufacturer of black ironmongery in the country and recognised by the trade as the best, in only fifteen years it had gone from zero to a leader of the industry. This is how the Chairman described their products: "*Every householder in England must use a product like that made by Duncombe's, whether it is to keep the mother-in-law out, or the rabbit or the pigeon in. Hasps and staples, tower bolts, brenton bolts, Suffolk latches, autogate latches to name a few…*"

The second of the latest purchases was **Heyes Lighting of Wigan**, specialising in making lights for hazardous areas. The demand for the lights that could be used safely in dangerous environments had been growing steadily, and this gave C&H a perfect opportunity to further fill their order book which, by then, was already looking as healthy as ever.

They seemed to have survived that particular economic winter spell. It looks like staying evergreen was all about balancing gains and losses, being flexible in pricing and design while strictly adhering to standards, but, mostly, it was about taking carefully calculated risks based on impeccable planning and scrupulous analysis of the situation. And, possibly, some luck.

It was rapidly getting warmer; the economic permafrost was thawing: "the Lawson boom" with its tax cuts increased people's disposable income and boosted consumer confidence. Oil, pumped out from under the North Sea, ran through the pipeline, along the way turning into sizable revenue. The economy grew. Government borrowing fell. Britain was now firmly embedded in the European Union. The communist regimes on the continent were beginning to crumble. Yes, it was definitely getting warmer. And yet, in people's minds, cutting through the understandable joy, rose a sobering question: how long will it last?

21

Sparkling in honour of sparks
(1990)

As the New Year approached, an old Abbahit from ten years before was again heard on every corner, raising the question: *"What lies waiting down the line In the end of eighty-nine?"* There would have been several possible answers, and the most obvious one, from the point of view of **Chamberlin and Hill Ltd**, was "a hundredth anniversary of the company". A whole century had passed since a much smaller, much dirtier, much more reliant on purely manual labour foundry in Walsall let out of its gate a horse-drawn cart loaded with the very first batch of castings. We don't know what exactly was in those initial containers, but in the first year of trading the sales turnover of C&H was £1,840 – more than a quarter of a million pounds in today's terms. Since then, regardless of the political and economic situation in the country, in times of abundance and scarcity, the company continued to make profit every year of its existence. And, as if by some deliberate arrangement, the record profit of £2,356,000 (5,33 million today) was achieved in the centenary year, giving the staff and management yet another good reason for celebration.

To mark the event, at the request of John Bather, the business's hundred-year-old logo was redesigned. The previous symbol, minimalist and clear – straight lines, angular letters resembling tools of the trade – was replaced by a more elaborate, almost exuberant image: the same two letters, but rounded and enclosed in a perfect circle echoing their outlines. The words "established 1890" appeared in small print inside the "C";

while seemingly nothing more than a modest statement of fact, this note said so much to those prepared to listen. From then on, this navy-blue circle would decorate the entrance of the company's main office at the Chuckery in Walsall as well as its official letters and documents.

And, of course, there was a party. A birthday party times a thousand. On a warm and dry day in June, employees from every company of the group were collected by coach and taken to a gala dinner at Catton Park in Derbyshire. There, on a vast lawn that looked as if it had been trimmed with some manicure scissors by hand, a larger-than-life marquee was erected, big enough to hold hundreds of people: all of the 584 C&H employees and their families were invited to attend. Food (shrimp cocktails, Coronation chicken and some deserts), wine (presumably, including that of a sparkling variety) and beer were served, and professional magicians made their rounds. Gold watches were presented to employees with twenty-five years of service; those who had worked for C&H for fifteen years received custom-made cufflinks. Later, the new company's logo appeared in the dark evening sky above the marquee: a spectacular firework display marked the end of the day that happens once in a century.

22

The swinging… nineties
(1991 – 1995)

While 1990 was an extraordinary year that would be remembered for the exceptional results achieved by C&H at the time of the economic recovery in the West Midlands, another round of recession was creeping in. Individual companies within the group reacted to the changing situation in different ways, and the only unifying feature of their performance in this period was the lack of a predictable pattern. For the next several years it appeared that all the parts of C&H were placed on some gigantic uncoordinated swings that kept oscillating between success and disappointment, never reaching, however, the point of real failure. In every annual report the Chairman would state significant differences in the results between the first and second half of that particular year as well as the differences in the productivity of each company.

Both foundries, the heart of the business, were performing less well than expected, but only slightly. In 1991, their production levels fell by 5%, and trading profits diminished by 6% compared to the previous year. However, the worrying trend continued, and in 1992, the trading profit was reduced to just over £1,000,000 (£1,857,325 today). This hadn't been caused by a loss of market share; in fact, C&H had acquired a great number of new customers. But the whole industry was functioning under a strain of ever more stringent environmental controls combined with difficulties experienced by the construction sector to which foundries had always been intrinsically linked, to a large extent mirroring its every fluctuation.

After the boom of the late 1980s, the recession in the beginning of 1990s hit the building trade hard, leading to the collapse of many companies. A slightly macabre joke, popular in that time, illustrated the state of the industry: *"What do you say to an architect with a job?" – "Big mac and fries, please!"* With a severely reduced demand, supply became more and more problematic. Bloxwich foundry, whose ties with the construction sector were particularly strong, was affected more than Chuckery. Luckily, after Britain had withdrawn from the ERM, both foundries' connections with their customers in continental Europe remained strong, and the direct exports contributed substantially to the companies' profits in the time when the domestic market was at a standstill. And yet in 1994, despite the Chuckery exceeding its sales as well as the profit budget and the export revenue rising from just below £2,000,000 to over £3,000,000, the low levels of activity at Bloxwich reduced the combined foundries' results by 19%. It looked like the later addition to the core business of C&H, their new engineering companies, had to be the main "breadwinner" from now on – or, at least, for now. How did they fare?

Petrel, the manufacturer of lighting designed to be used in hazardous areas, had been slowly restoring its order book after a setback caused by an unfortunate acquisition, two years prior, of the Heyes lighting range that fell below the standards C&H's customers expected. By 1993, **Petrel** managed to increase its trading profits and was striving to restore the lost margins to their pre-Heyes level. In 1994, this aim was achieved as a result of an improved and growing range of cost-effective products fully meeting all the certification requirements of its international and domestic clients.

Fred Duncombe was the only division of C&H that, despite being equally connected to the construction industry, in 1991 succeeded not only in simply keeping the previously achieved momentum but also in increasing, against all the odds, the turnover and trading profit by 20%. The following year was as successful, and the decision to increase its manufacturing capacity was taken. The company received new equipment which enabled it to extend the range of its products.

By now, all the increase in group profits came from C&H's engineering companies, even if in different proportions. At the beginning of the new decade, **Conduit Fittings** and **Fitter and Poulton**, suppliers of components to the electrical installations market, experienced a severe downturn in their activity. Here again, in the words of the Chairman, *"the virtual* *disappearance of new construction contracts took its toll"*. An immediate action to substantially reduce the production costs was required, and in 1991 both businesses were consolidated onto one site. The move was expensive (about £100,000 had been charged against the group's profits), but necessary to ensure that the company was well prepared for the time when the situation on the market changed for the better. The expected benefits followed but were short-lived: in 1992, the trading profit improved by a third, only to drop by 10% below that in the following year. The metaphorical swing continued its unstoppable motion.

23

The black side of the
White House
(1996)

I f the situation on the domestic market was far from ideal, the export
sales continued to thrive. It would be impossible (and unnecessary) now
to try and trace all the products that found their way from the factories
of C&H to their overseas customers, but one particular order deserves
mentioning here, and this is why.

On 4th October 1993, the White House was encircled by the Russian
Army. No, this didn't happen in Washington. Moscow has its very own
White House, a government building situated in the centre of the capital.
After a prolonged confrontation between the president of Russia and
its Parliament, the former ordered the military to seize the latter. In the
early hours of that freezing cold Monday, tanks of the Red Army's elite
Taman Division began shelling the Bely Dom. The whole world saw the
striking photographs of the building, once elegantly monumental and
imposing, later mortally wounded and covered in gaping black holes.
Inside it didn't look any better. In just a few days, order in the city was
restored and, eventually, the time came to repair the mutilated Residence
of Democracy, Russian edition.

In 1996, the Turkish company **GAMA Industries** was awarded the
contract to repair the building. They had nine months to complete the
whole project. Pressed for time, they turned to **Fitter and Poulton Ltd**
which had developed an innovative and unique Click-Fit conduit system
that could be joined in seconds instead of hours, the traditional process of

connecting the malleable casting would have taken. C&H's flexible conduit tubing came in rolls where the thin metal core was covered in plastic coating. A small blade in the pressed conduit box cut into the core, earthing it through the tubular system, as the regulations of that time required.

For completing the renovation of the White House right on schedule and to the highest standards, **GAMA Industries** received a "Certificate of Honour" from the Russian Government. Technically, the contribution of **Fitter and Poulton** to this success might not seem that substantial: after all, they only supplied one specific part out of many required. However, it was an important segment of the building's electric circuit allowing it to function smoothly and efficiently which, in turn, created a perfect working environment for the newly elected Russian Parliament.

Gordon told me about this episode from C&H's biography at the very first of our meetings, and I knew immediately that this was something I had to write about. I was in Moscow that unforgettable autumn of 1996. The gloom of those days had been matched by the hope grown out of the despair, and I wanted to mention the contribution, however small, that C&H had made toward the restoration of normality in the city torn between its own past and future. But by the time I reached the right point in the narrative, the world had changed. The building where the entire electrical system was functioning, thanks to the clever device invented and supplied by **Fitter and Poulton**, now housed a nest of vipers endorsing and justifying the war against a neighbouring country started by the Kremlin Psychopath. The story behind that particular product manufactured by C&H nearly thirty years ago had suddenly lost its appeal.

And yet here it is. Events don't get erased from history simply because they are not mentioned. Facts remain facts regardless of their future interpretations. C&H designed and produced an innovative appliance that allowed them to successfully compete on the international market and that helped the restoration of an important governmental building in Moscow. That's all that matters. Thousands of companies around the world invested in projects in the country that had been taking tentative steps towards democracy. As for a u-turn in its course which, decades later, this country chose to take – well, that's on Russia.

But let's move on. On the whole, both profit and turnover increased in 1996, mainly due to the performance of the foundries. But the success was, in the words of the Chairman, "*tempered by a continuing margin squeeze resulting from higher operating costs not being recovered from customers".* To support the cost reduction programme, a modern cope and drag line was installed in Walsall replacing some outdated equipment. Similar advancement was planned for Bloxwich. The engineering companies were focused on the development of new products, including a range of fluorescent lighting for hazardous areas. **Fred Duncombe** extended the scope of its emergency exit hardware. The market was being monitored closely, and no efforts were spared to stop the swing from going too far in the wrong direction.

24

Milieu of the new millennium
(1997 – 2005)

Around the turn of the millennium, it looked like they had succeeded in that quest. For the next several years every annual chairman's report began with the acknowledgement of the improved results achieved by the group. Barrie Williams, then the Chief Executive of C&H, explained the cause of the misfortunes in the recent past: *"Chamberlin and Hill was at one time identified as a cyclical company in jobbing markets…"*

The idea was quite simple. Inevitably, C&H had always been tightly integrated into the UK's – and, by extension, the wider world's – economy. Economies develop in a cyclical pattern, going through expansion, peak, contraction and trough. Any company operating within this system would experience the effects of each of these stages. While it was impossible to avoid the downturns altogether, being proactive and attempting to minimise the negative consequences of the systemic recession was certainly within the capabilities (and a sign) of good management. Successful damage limitation would allow a company to break out of the cycle. And that was what Barrie Williams set out to do, reorganising the business in order to amplify the progress during the favourable conditions and cushion the slumps in hard times. From his report: *"we owned four foundries in no way as focused as our present two, nor anywhere near as well equipped…*

Alongside this transformation we have been investing in engineering product development to serve the safety and security markets. There is organic potential growth in these markets, and if we can find West Midlands companies for sale in the same market area we will make acquisitions… As we see it, we have no sensible alternative but to continue with an aggressive policy of improvement."

In 1998, C&H sold a part of the site of **Fitter and Poulton** raising £155,000 that contributed to that year's profit of £2,731,000 (£4,280,788 today). At the end of that year they purchased **Ductile Castings Limited**, a company based in Scunthorpe and producing high quality grey and alloy castings used in turbines and vacuum pumps. Now the group consisted of three foundries instead of two, and two engineering companies instead of three (**Fitter and Poulton** and **Petrel** had been consolidated into **PFP Electrical Products**), creating a business with a better defined structure and with more specialised and focused constituents.

Expanding the group was not the only reason for acquiring new companies. In 1999, C&H purchased **Webb Lloyd Ltd**, a maker of hardware door furniture and a known competitor of C&H's own **Fred Duncombe**. With the company came its customer base, substantially expanding the order book of C&H.

The strategy seemed to be working – or mostly working: at the end of 2000, the chairman's report stated *"in the last five years profits have doubled, earnings have risen from 14.14p to 26.67p and the dividend by close to 50%. The fact that sales have only risen by about 18% over the same period can be seen as strength rather than the reverse, because we have become increasingly competitive in markets which demand the continuous improvement culture which we pursue. Yet the share price has not shown commensurable progress."*

As a company, **Chamberlin and Hill Ltd** was intrinsically linked with the foundry business and, as such, according to Barrie Williams, *"was seen as '"old economy' and therefore unlikely or even unable to grow shareholder value at a reasonable rate".* That was hardly surprising: in people's minds, the very word "foundry" was associated with something right out of a Dickens novel, synonymous with "outdated", "tough", even "gruelling". It wasn't sexy enough. And it wasn't twenty-first century enough. Yes, the world now lived not simply in a new year – it lived in a new century. Forget the century – it lived in the new millennium! People were acutely aware of that fact. They wanted to invest in something more fitting with the times. And the times, it seemed, were better matched with the technology from books by Isaac Asimov than from those of Charles Dickens.

The times called for clever computers and dexterous robots. Those were incompatible with a foundry, right?

Not quite. In 2001, **Chamberlin and Hill Ltd** purchased Koyama's Barinder grinding machines and installed them in Walsall and Bloxwich. Those were Japanese manufactured, easily programmable robotic grinders operating within the tolerance of 0.5 mm. C&H was the first company outside the Land of the Rising Sun to use them in their foundries. Before, castings had been ground manually: a labour-intensive and time-consuming procedure. What's more, workers operating such machines had often sustained injuries caused by continuous vibration. Simple auto grinders existed even then, but were very inefficient and cumbersome to use. The machine developed by Koyama was different. It was equipped with a high precision CNC (Computer Numerical Control) technology as well as a Barinder diamond grinding wheel which lasted up to twenty times longer than its carborundum predecessor of the traditional device. These intelligent grinders had been widely used in Japan, but were not really known in the rest of the world. Paul Smith, Koyama's representative in the UK, travelled up and down the country trying to find a British foundry that would be willing to take the risk of buying the innovative machine. He found such a company in the West Midlands. Barrie Williams from **Chamberlin and Hill Ltd** sensed its potential. He and two general managers from Walsall and Bloxwich went to Japan to see the device in action… and were not allowed into the foundry where it was operating! Did the Japanese suspect that the trio from the UK were industrial spies or were they simply observing their strict "staff only" policy? I don't know. But in the end, Barrie won. The little delegation from C&H entered the premises, watched the wonder machine perform its magic and were convinced. They purchased five grinders, two for Bloxwich and three for Walsall, and returned to the UK, followed shortly by their Japanese colleagues who helped install the new lines and train the staff. And, just like that, within weeks, a near-Dickensian set-up was replaced by a super-modern arrangement. The same guys who used to perform some of the most exhausting and dirtiest jobs in the foundry, became robotic machine operators, stopping short of wearing white lab coats. They inspected the castings for imperfections and placed them into the device which now did the rest: grinding, fettling and gauging if required – twenty-first century style.

The next global slowdown, as predicted by the economists, was already descending on the developed world, swallowing one state after another. Signs of it were beginning to be felt in the UK, although this country managed to resist the fully blown recession until the late 2000s. C&H reacted to the impending complications by stepping up their "aggressive policy of improvement". In April 2004, another business, **Russell Castings** of Leicester, was purchased and added to the group, expanding its foundry division. At the General Meeting a year later, the Chairman described it as *"the largest contributor to the Group's welcome return to growth"* which *"continues to demonstrate it was a solid investment"*.

And, with that successful business deal, C&H's long and fruitful Era of Acquisitions came to an end. But the story continued…

Supplement for Part IV:
Simply Statistics

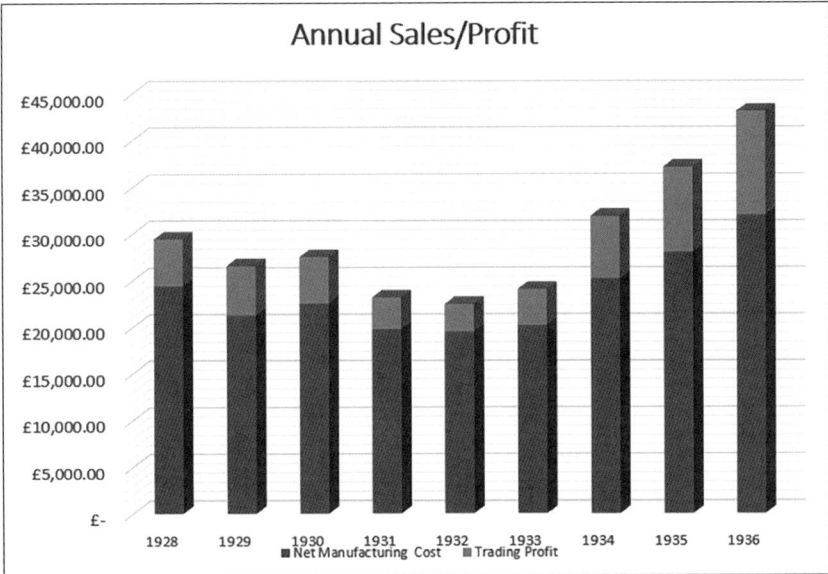

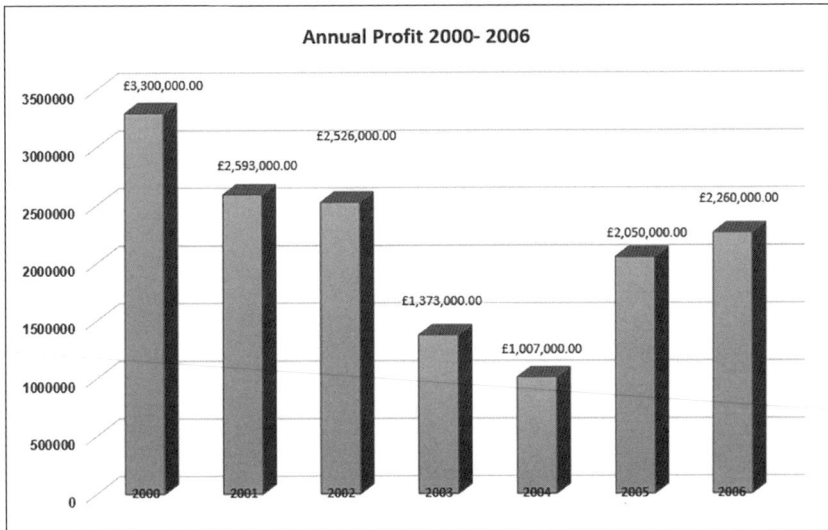

Annual Sales/Profit

	1928	1929	1930	1931	1932	1933	1934	1935	1936

■ Net Manufacturing Cost ■ Trading Profit

(Y-axis: £-, £5,000.00, £10,000.00, £15,000.00, £20,000.00, £25,000.00, £30,000.00, £35,000.00, £40,000.00, £45,000.00)

Annual Profit 2000- 2006

Year	Profit
2000	£3,300,000.00
2001	£2,593,000.00
2002	£2,526,000.00
2003	£1,373,000.00
2004	£1,007,000.00
2005	£2,050,000.00
2006	£2,260,000.00

HISTORY OF
CHAMBERLIN AND HILL

PART

5

25

To switch off Bloxwich
(2006)

One sunny (cloudy, rainy, stormy) evening in the early (late) spring (summer, autumn, winter) of 2006, a bittersweet party was held in the Grosvenor room of Blakenall Football Club grounds on the border of Walsall and Bloxwich. I couldn't give a more precise account of it (hence the "multiple choice" descriptions in brackets) because it is not mentioned in the official documents I have studied, and not a single person of those who attended the event came forward to share memories. All I managed to find out was that the entire workforce of the Bloxwich foundry and their family members had been invited, and drinks had been plentiful and totally free of charge. Here ends the "sweet" part. Now for the "bitter" one: this was a "leaving do" organised for (and by) the workers of the Bloxwich plant. It didn't take place within the foundry walls because those walls were not to stand there for much longer: the foundry that had been an integral part of **Chamberlin and Hill Ltd** for thirty-nine years, in 2006 was about to be demolished. It had just been sold to a construction company erecting houses across the road from the plant; having run out of grounds to build on, this company fancied C&H's site. As it happens, C&H, at that particular time, fancied some cash. So this seemed to be a match made in business deal heaven. Just one question, though: why would a company as large and successful as C&H, whose Chairman reported a 103% increase in profits and a growth of 54% at the end of the previous financial year, need money badly enough to have to sell one of its most important assets?

At the time, the asset in question, the Bloxwich foundry, had indeed been trading successfully – but this success was mostly due to a lucrative contract with its biggest customer, Swiss group **Georg Fisher**. In 2006, the Swiss decided to move their business to Slovakia, leaving a large hole in the foundry's order book – a hole that would have been impossible to patch up fast enough. Meanwhile, another gap in the company's accounts became apparent: the "pension pot" was found to be underfunded. This wasn't a problem affecting exclusively C&H, but a fate of many businesses: having employed a financial adviser responsible specifically for their pension fund, they realised later that the expert had not handled it well, not necessarily due to some ill intent or lack of professionalism. The required calculations were very complex and involved a large number of variables, some of which were not easy to determine. In the case of C&H, by 2006 the pension pot was found to be 7% short of the expected £10,000,000. So when the representative of the building firm turned up on the foundry's doorstep with a very reasonable offer, it was readily accepted. This was a simple, carefully considered and mutually beneficial deal between two companies. From C&H's perspective, this transaction was flawless: getting rid of the division in danger of becoming a liability, the management aimed to strengthen the rest of the group. All the restructuring costs caused by the loss of the foundry were more than covered with the exceptional gain of £1.03m from the sale of the site.

But, of course, a business – any business – is more than the sum of its assets (however valuable), the product it generates (however important), and the cash it injects into the country's economy (however generously). It's also about the people who work there, without whom these assets would be nothing more than piles of bricks and lumps of metal. So, while the decision to sell the foundry did make perfect sense from the point of view of the company's bookkeeping, for the staff of the foundry its closure was a significant, in many cases life altering, event. The majority of staff had been made redundant. Fifteen out of about 150 had been offered jobs in the Chuckery. I spoke with one of them, Andy Holden, at the very beginning of my research. "*This was a sad, nasty time,*" he remembered, "*people felt very, very bitter and resentful. They took the redundancy money and went their way.*" He himself seemed to have done well despite, if not because of, the move. Now the superintendent of the finishing department in Walsall, Andy was to give me a tour around the foundry, appearing confident and happy. But what about those who did not get re-hired in another of C&H's foundries? Well, I can't tell: nobody was available for an interview.

26

Chamberlin loses Hill…
(2007 – 2009)

No-one knew then that the sale of the Bloxwich foundry marked the beginning of a very different period in the history of **Chamberlin and Hill Ltd**. Tim Hair, who in 2007 replaced Barrie Williams as the Chief Executive Officer, had his own and very different idea of how to run the business of which he was now in charge. Apart from anything else, his vision involved the change of the group's name. Soon after his appointment, at one of the board meetings he suggested that the surname of only one of the two Victorian gentlemen who had built the whole enterprise should be included in its name. So they dropped Hill. From 2nd of August 2007, the group was to be called **Chamberlin Plc**.

"What's in a name", right? With or without Mr Hill's presence in the title, the foundries of the group would have continued to spit molten iron from the throats of their insanely hot furnaces; the engineering companies would have carried on producing the electrical installations and security hardware. The only place where this change would have become evident was the official documentation in which the group's name would have been replaced with its revised, shorter version. If anything, this would have resulted in an economy of ink – surely a positive development?

Obviously, it's highly unlikely that saving on printing essentials was on Tim Hair's mind when he made his decision. But what was? What compelled the newly appointed CEO to change the over-a-century old tradition and seemingly randomly remove the mention of one of the company's founders – the very one who was actually a founder (pun intended) – from that company's name? I asked Gordon. He shrugged: *"Who knows? We didn't really understand the point of it then. Maybe he thought it sounded better that way. He convinced all the other directors easily. He knew how to present ideas."* Trying to ask the man himself was not any more helpful: I emailed him and sent letters to both his home and business addresses, asking for an interview, and got no reply. So we will never know. But today the foundry part of the group is still called **Chamberlin and Hill Castings Ltd**. And this is what the whole enterprise is associated with. So, maybe in a slight breach of the strictest rules of business bureaucracy, I think of the company as (and write about the history) of **Chamberlin and Hill Ltd**, paying tribute to both of its "fathers". May the mighty Gods of Entrepreneurship forgive me for this well-meaning liberty. However, for the sake of historical accuracy, from now on I must stick to the official name, **Chamberlin Plc**, when talking about the whole group.

One of the reasons Tim Hair was selected for the job was simple. An ex-director of a company producing hydraulics, he was expected to bring his expertise and experience of a non-foundry-related industry to C&H. And this, according to the chairman's report of the same year, was what the management wanted: *"The board has concluded that it is desirable to re-balance the Group by expanding our engineering activities, largely by acquisition, creating a more broadly based engineering group."* It began to look like the company that had started off as a single foundry and for decades had remained an important part of the sector was ready to recreate itself as a very different enterprise. Was it possible that, in time, they were planning to leave the foundry business altogether? Here is my very own mini-conspiracy theory: the name of Henry Hill, the original foundry man, "Adam of Chuckery", was deleted from the company's name as a symbolic gesture indicating the forthcoming change, signalling the move away from the foundry business… okay, I think I have gone too far here. Back to the real world.

And the real world was not feeling well, displaying some worrying symptoms: its physical temperature steadily rising, its economy experiencing serious chills and fatigue. The Great Recession of the early 2000s, which had grown out of the financial crisis in the USA, was steadily spreading all over the planet, infecting one developed country after another. The recession had already begun to gnaw at the British economy while the board of C&H's directors Chamberlin and Hill were implementing changes in the company's policy.

The integration of the Bloxwich foundry's workload into the Chuckery was completed; all the light castings (those under 5 kg) were now produced in Walsall and used, to a large extent, by the automotive supply chain. Heavier castings continued to be made in Scunthorpe and Leicester. All three foundries were doing well and gaining new clients; there was no shortage of orders. But the prices of raw materials, especially pig iron and steel scrap, had risen sharply. It became impossible to absorb the costs without passing some of them on to the customers. The prices were soaring, the purchasing power of consumers was heading down even faster. The strong demand the foundries experienced in early 2008 plummeted later in the year, and this reduction was made worse by the destocking of the supply chains.

In a stable economy, while the trading conditions are sunny, it is a common practice of many prudent companies to squirrel away a sensible amount of essential stocks "for a rainy day". When such a day inevitably comes, they start using these reserves – "destocking" – which allows them to continue working without the need of buying more of the stocks and still achieving the same results. Say, if a company had been purchasing certain castings from **Chamberlin Plc** on a regular basis and using them to make its own products, it would have deliberately accumulated enough of these castings to stop buying the new ones if their price went up, and still have enough supplies to be able to function. And in 2008 it seemed to be raining non-stop, regardless of the season…

Of course, destocking and other calamitous consequences of the recession affected not only the foundry part of the business. Walsall and Leicester were particularly badly hit and lost over 50% of orders from some of their customers, while, to quote the chairman's report, "*the engineering businesses, which account for approximately 17% of total revenues, were affected less significantly but they also experienced reduced demand.*" The UK's government simply had no means to invest in technological projects; the country's population had no money to buy non-essential hi-tech goods like cars. Luckily, the sales of the group were not overly concentrated on any single part of the market with the most significant, as stated in the report, "*being passenger cars (13% of sales), construction equipment (12%), commercial vehicles (12%) and hydraulics (9%)*". This breadth of the customer base cushioned the downfall. Still, the autumn of 2009, "*saw the most dramatic decline in the engineering economy in modern times and the second half of the last year proved to be extremely difficult*".

The management had to take measures to minimise the inevitable impact of the recession on the business. Back in September 2008, in anticipation of the difficulties ahead, the board of directors came up with some tough plans. Again, let's see how the Chairman explained them in his report: "*Although the extent of the downturn was beyond our expectations, these plans, which included redundancies, short time working at all sites, wage freezes and rigorous spending control, allowed an immediate reaction to the downturn and limited the damage to the business.*" A few short lines, clinically clear and self-explanatory; behind them – tales of anxiety and hardship, of distorted destinies, real-life stories worthy of Dickens's quill, adjusted to the reality of the twenty-first century… But no, I am not trying to pin a heavy load of guilt onto the collective consciousness of **Chamberlin's** management. Had they not done what they did, the whole group could have ceased to exist, and this would have been far, far worse for anyone involved. The solution to the problem of keeping the business afloat under the most challenging circumstances was a convoluted jigsaw of difficult decisions, each of which was necessary to complete the puzzle. But there is one small thing that I don't understand, one tiny piece of evidence that doesn't seem to fit into this otherwise coherently and successfully constructed jigsaw: the fact that, according to the company's own records, during the time of that "*rigorous spending control*", the time of lost jobs and frozen wages, the time of shared tangible austerity, the salary of the new CEO escalated from a highly comfortable "five-star" £192,000 which his just-retired predecessor Barrie Williams had been receiving, to a "presidential suite" luxurious £226,000; a year later it would jump to £253,000. Then again, my own knowledge of how to run a business equals precisely zero, so this pay increase might have been perfectly justified and I am wrong in finding it a little surprising. Am I?

Directors' salaries aside, the policy of careful manoeuvring around the potential explosives on the minefield of the recession-bruised economy delivered unexpectedly good results: by the end of a difficult 2009, the profit before tax, excluding the exceptional items, went up to £1.4million: an improvement of 27% on the previous year; earnings per share rose by 44%.

27

… and profit
(2010)

Meanwhile, the country was slowly emerging from the tenacious grips of the crisis, promising a new lease of life to all the dormant businesses around. It would be tempting to say that for **Chamberlin Plc**, too, a swift recovery from the downturn was to follow. But the company's records tell us a different, and unexpected, story.

In 2010, at the traditional annual meeting, CEO Tim Hair presented his report containing, for the first time in over a century of the company's history, the word "loss": *"the Group delivered an underlying operating loss of £923,000 against an underlying operating profit of £460,000 last year."* At that stage, no major disaster had hit the company – and yet, **Chamberlin Plc**, which had seemed to have sailed through every single hard period until now, achieved its worst result in the year when the economy-on-the-mend had stopped throwing nasty challenges around. Reading the report, I tried to gauge the level of distress this would have caused those in charge of the company, and found that the tone of the text in front of me was not at all gloomy. One particular sentence caught my attention: *"Chamberlin has been rested by recession and emerged strongly."* Did it really imply that the period of stagnation in the economy and all the problems that it inflicted onto the company – absence of orders, restricted capacity of factories, numerous redundancies – instead of damaging the business, provided it with a respite? A respite from… success? From profitability? That didn't make sense. I began to understand what Gordon had meant when he mentioned "the CEO of the day's" incredible powers of persuasion (or, at least, his ability to convey undesirable information in a way that would make it a lot more palatable). In reality, the situation must have been bleak and anxiety-inducing; the report draped an intricate and prepossessing verbal pattern over it, either as a means of distraction from the possible management failures (see the graph illustrating the dynamics of the company's profit at around this time), or simply as a way of instilling a much needed optimistic attitude into the members of the board.

The remedy for the situation took the form of some reorganisation within the group. This was the result: in the foundry division, the Scunthorpe plant specialising in manufacturing very heavy, low volume castings was assigned its own dedicated management team. It was one of only two foundries in the UK with the capacity to cast up to six tonnes of high-grade iron. The Leicester plant, producing medium weight, lower volume castings, was brought under the control of **Chamberlin and Hill Castings** that also managed Chuckery in Walsall, the original foundry whose speciality had always been smaller parts with complex internal passages.

The engineering part of the business, **Fred Duncombe**, was now called **Exidor**: a suitable name for a business specialising in making emergency exit hardware such as crash bars fitted to fire escape doors. Under normal conditions, these doubled up as a security feature providing protection against break-ins. The range of **Exidor's** products was extended further after the acquisition of designs and some of the stocks from **Jebron Ltd,** a company that had manufactured door closers but went into administration during the recession.

The third division, **Petrel**, didn't undergo any significant structural changes. This company producing lighting and controls for hazardous environments retained its strong position in the highly regulated market that had been largely unaffected by the recession. **Petrel's** sales team was strengthened to include an experienced agent to cover a territory in Germany: their customer base had been steadily expanding.

There weren't many businesses around that could have boasted a loss-free run as long as that of **Chamberlin Plc**. Come to think of it, there weren't many businesses around, profitable or otherwise, that had simply existed for as long as **Chamberlin Plc**. A bad year – one out of 120! – was not going to knock the group off its place on the country's industrial landscape or damage its reputation. It only meant that in 2010 **Chamberlin Plc**, formerly known as **Chamberlin and Hill Ltd**, ceased to be this unique creature, this pristinely white unicorn, and joined the rest of the business world notorious for its zebra-like pattern of profit and loss…

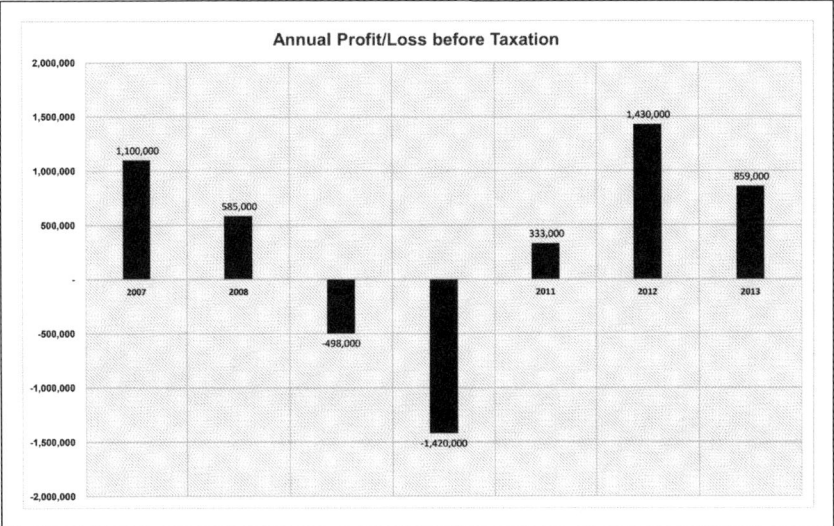

Dynamics of the company's profit Graph

28

Back in the black
(2011 – 2013)

L uckily, the first dark stripe in Chamberlin's zebra happened to be no more than just a streak. In the decade preceding the recession, most European and American companies had transferred production to Eastern countries like China or India where the labour costs had been significantly lower. The end of the global downturn was marked by a very welcome reversal of that economic model. Manufacturing started to return to the West, and **Chamberlin Plc** became one of the beneficiaries of this "homecoming". Its order book was filling up again.

The same diversity that had helped the company not to sink during the recession enabled it to find solid ground during the recovery. **Chamberlin Plc** served a whole range of markets, including hydraulics, mining, hazardous environment power generation and construction equipment. However, the focus of the group's activity at the time was on the automotive industry.

In 2011, over 20% of all sales in the foundry division were made up of turbocharger castings. These were produced in Chuckery which happened to be one of only four specialist foundries in Europe with the technical capability to manufacture such parts. Fortunately for **Chamberlin Plc**, the global trend to supply new petrol car engines with turbochargers was getting stronger, driven by strict emissions regulations. A turbocharger, installed in the exhaust of a vehicle, made it significantly more efficient: a 1.2 litre motor equipped with such a device delivered the same output as a 1.6

litre engine. In 2010, only 10% of all petrol engines had been turbocharged; in just four years this figure was expected to rise to 90%. It appeared that the Chuckery was not about to run out of orders – and so it didn't. In 2011, the Walsall foundry was operating at 100% of its pre-recession volume.

Leicester was less successful in restoring its full capacity, but, as its major customer, the construction industry, was recovering from the downturn, so was the foundry. It specialised in producing mid-size technologically complex iron castings designed to have high strength and corrosion, wear, or low temperature resistance. The demand for such castings was on the increase.

By the end of 2011, the process of combining the management of the two foundries, started a year earlier, was successfully completed and delivered significant reduction in overheads.

The Scunthorpe foundry, **Russell Ductile Casting**, experienced an impressive surge in demand, exceeding its pre-recession levels in 2012. To a large extent such gain was achieved due to the order from **Howdens**, a firm based in Glasgow, which used **RDC**'s castings as components in specialist compressors they manufactured for their end customer, **Queensland Gas (QCG)** of Australia. During the downturn these castings operations had been reconfigured to improve efficiency: that, paired with the peaking sales, promised significant profits.

The engineering companies, **Exidor** and **Petrel**, did not lag behind the foundries in improving their results. In 2012, the Group's revenues rose by 14% to £45m (over £52m today), and underlying operating profit increased by 92% to £17m (nearly £20m). **Chamberlin Plc** was back in the black – which, ironically, meant that the black stripe the company had been going through was officially over. But the significance of these few years in the group's history goes beyond the return to profitability. An important development was taking place in Chuckery.

A couple of lines in the 2013 chairman's report – *"we are currently installing a new process in our Walsall foundry which will deliver attractive ongoing cost reductions"* – didn't really capture my attention. Technological novelties had been introduced into the group's factories almost all the time; mentioning every single one of them would have made the size of my book closer to that of the Encyclopaedia Britannica, so I was about to ignore this. But I was wrong. *"It needs to be acknowledged,"* said Gordon, *"it has opened a whole new era for the foundry. They started cleaning castings on the site."*

"Cleaning castings", in a foundry's terms, means first sandblasting and then dipping them into a container filled with sodium hydroxide, more universally known as lye or caustic soda. It used to be done externally, involving complicated logistics and additional costs. In 2013, that changed. The cleaning station was introduced to the finishing department of Chuckery, allowing for the whole process of making a casting, from melting the metal to dispatching the ready product, to be conducted in the foundry. (I have seen the area and had a tour around the department: a short interview with its supervisor, Andy Holden, will follow a few pages later.)

The best equipment in the world would have been useless without qualified, experienced and dedicated staff. Investing in training and personnel had always been an important part of the group's policy. In the absence of a national programme for foundry-specific higher education, **Chamberlin Plc** felt the need *"to increase the number of skilled casting engineers and craftsmen"*. The group had already been running, on and off for some twenty years, various programmes allowing university students to have working experience in its foundries. One of the participants, Adam Vicary, came to Chuckery in the eighties as a graduate and stayed there. He went on to become Technical Manager of Bloxwich, gradually progressing to the position of Managing Director of **Ductile Castings**, then Managing Director of **Chamberlin and Hill Castings Ltd** and, finally, a Group Director of **Chamberlin Plc**. Such schemes, undeniably useful, nevertheless lacked regularity and structure. To remedy this, in 2012, **Chamberlin Plc** in conjunction with the industry's professional body, the **Institute of Cast Metals Engineers (ICME)**, established a casting foundation degree qualification to prepare the next generation of casting engineers.

The newly created graduate scheme consisted of two different types of work placement. The first one included a year of work in the industry and was offered to an undergraduate as part of the degree or to a graduate student as targeted work experience. The second was a two-year Professional Excellence and Leadership Development Programme for qualified graduates who, on successful completion of the course, could get a permanent job within **Chamberlin Plc**.

The first group of four students, two for each type of placement, were recruited from Birmingham University. They were sent to Walsall and Leicester foundries to work on projects which involved production technology, process engineering, metallurgical control, subcontractor assessment, machining, lead time matrix, costs and budgeting and vendor management systems.

We tried but could not trace those pioneers, but this is what the chairman's report says about them: "*In doing this scheme we have gained professional, high level problem solvers with enthusiasm and a state of the art, fresh way of thinking. The graduates have been heavily involved in the new process implementation at Walsall… They have brought vitality, a new insight into age-old problems and have had a positive effect on the overall culture of the business. The graduate scheme is something we will continue into the future to ensure we have a steady supply of talent entering the Group.*"

With fresh talent, new equipment and up-to-date technologies flowing in, it appeared that **Chamberlin Plc** had everything it needed to leave behind the unfortunate slip and continue its unblemished, loss-free existence in the future.

29

"Le Rouge et le Noir" (for the lack of a more original title)
(2014 – 2016)

But expectations don't always match reality.

In 2014, the economy was slowing down again, and the demand for castings, particularly the larger ones, dropped dramatically; as a result, the foundry division saw a 14% downturn in sales. In itself, this would not have made a major dent in the group's accounts, but that particular year was plagued by a series of unfortunate events and circumstances. The Leicester foundry experienced severe operational difficulties: one of their customers, **J C Bamford**, or **JCB**, reduced their annual order from two to just half a million pounds. As if this wasn't bad enough, technical problems crippled some of the equipment. Due to the machines' downtime, the scrap rates of manufacture soared while the efficiency plummeted. All the urgent "rescue measures" set the group back by half a million pounds. And this was not the only exceptional cost **Chamberlin Plc** had to bear. Added to it was £690,000 spent on restructuring within the group. During the second half of the year, the three foundries were brought together under single management. In the long run this would guarantee reduced expenses, but in the meantime it increased the financial burden. A further £307,000 was paid out to cover the contractual obligations to the former CEO, Tim Hair, who had just left his position, and for the recruitment of his successor, Kevin Nolan. These exceptionally high exceptional costs were the main contributor to the loss of £0.8 million sustained by the group in 2014. **Chamberlin Plc** was in the red again. Its triumphant return to the golden era of never-trading-at-a-loss failed to materialise. Frankly, remaining constantly profitable would have been hardly possible in this tempestuous century prone to so much social, political and economic turbulence; however, minimising the negative impact of the losses on the company and finding efficient ways of returning to successful trading was well within the remit of its management.

Early in 2015, the positive impact of the restructuring within the group began to be felt. At the same time, the turbocharger bearing market showed clear signs of recovery which, in turn, boosted the performance of Chuckery. In the autumn two major contracts were signed whose end customer was **Jaguar** in Bradford. With an increased number of orders flowing in, the Walsall foundry swiftly became profitable again. According to the chairman's report, so did the engineering companies. No details were given in the document about what had been the driving force behind the improvement, but a short paragraph demonstrated that the recovery had, indeed, taken place: *"Revenues increased by 5.9% to £40.8 million, and the Group has returned to profitability with a £1.6 million turnaround, posting underlying profit before tax of 0.8 million against a loss of 0.8 million in the prior year"*. **Chamberlin Plc** yet again reversed its trajectory.

Being profitable certainly made it easier to continue the programme of improvement within the group. In 2016, this took the form of introducing machining facilities to **Chamberlin and Hill Ltd**. An American company, **BorgWarner**, one of the twenty-five largest automotive suppliers in the world that happened to be a customer of **Chamberlin's**, had suggested this to the group's management and even had assisted them in getting all the necessary equipment. For a curious but uninitiated observer like me this might seem a bit odd: how can "introducing machining facilities" be considered a new development in a place already bursting with heavy machinery?

Machining is a process that finishes… a finished casting. Initially, I was under the impression that a product leaving the finishing department of a foundry becomes just that: a finished product. Hence the name. But nothing in this life is ever so easy. While castings piled up in the corner of this department are, indeed, ready to be sent off to the customer, they cannot be used there straight from the container immediately upon arrival. They need to be customised. Certain adjustments have to be made to them in order for the castings to be fitted into more complex structures and to function as they are supposed to. The process of creating an object by pouring molten metal into even the most elaborate mould has its limitations: it doesn't allow for the desired degree of precision, and therefore every surface of a casting is always made just a little bigger than required. Later this extra material – the machining allowance – will have to be "shaved off", bringing the "freshly manufactured" object in line with the specifications. As a result, a casting in its new and final reincarnation will be different from its "just out of the foundry" version. Machining is the procedure which enables this reincarnation to take place. All of **Chamberlin's** customers had the necessary equipment to do this on their own premises. For decades such an arrangement had been working just fine for everybody involved; however, the value of the group's product would have increased significantly if one of the foundries could add machining to the list of its services. And so in 2016 they did. **Chamberlin Plc** became the only fully integrated supplier of grey iron bearing housing in Europe.

The new £2.1m facility with an annual capacity of 750,000 parts was placed in a warehouse about one and a half miles from the Chuckery. It was tuned to machining of the most profitable product of the foundry, the turbochargers' components, and consisted of three purpose-built appliances linked by sequenced conveyor systems that carried the castings from one operation to the next. During this circumnavigation each casting would have acquired all the properties that could not have been achieved by the moulding process alone.

Awareness of the ecological damage caused by the ever-increasing number of vehicles on the roads all over the planet grew as fast as the industry itself, pressing manufacturers to implement environmentally friendlier technologies and to develop greener products. Here is where this turbocharger housing that I have mentioned before comes in.

A turbocharger is an important part of an automotive engine, allowing it to function a lot more efficiently. It consists of three parts: a turbine (or a "hot side") where the rotational power is produced, a compressor which pressurises the air drawn in from the outside, and the centre housing that accommodates the shaft connecting the first two. The housing also contains a bearing filled with lubrication oil minimising the rotational friction of the shaft and consequently boosting the engine's performance. This system was perfectly suited to diesel powered motors (and by the early twenty-first century all such vehicles had been equipped with turbochargers), but not so much to petrol cars. The shafts in petrol turbos rotate much faster than in diesel ones, heating the lubricant to unsafe levels. Without a turbocharger, a car engine cannot perform to its full potential, wasting fuel and creating extra pollution. In an era when the word "green" means a lot more than just a colour, this presented a serious problem. **BorgWarner** (let's remember this name: it will come up again and again in this story), the same company on whose request a machining plant had been installed in Chuckery, came up with the idea of cooling the oil inside the turbo, and brought some drawings of the proposed innovation to **Chamberlin Plc** hoping that they would be able to find a way of "translating" the image into a casting – which they did. A team at Walsall manufactured turbine housing made of very robust cast iron and featuring a water runner structure that protected the lubricant from overheating, regardless of the rotational speed of the shaft. Such housings were perfect for petrol engines. And Chuckery, with its brand new machining plant, was perfect for producing those perfect parts.

While the latest addition to the group's assets had opened exciting long-term possibilities, the immediate results were less encouraging: the demand in the core markets was waning; prices of oil, gas and steel were creeping up. In addition, sterling grew stronger, which directly affected **Chamberlin Plc** since nearly one third of all its sales were denominated in euros. Consequently, and taking into account the restructuring costs, in 2016 the group lost £0.2m before tax. In 2015, they had generated a profit of £0.1m. So it appeared that careful balancing between being in the red and in the black became **Chamberlin's** new reality.

30

Exidor exits the Leicester-less Group
(2017 – 2019)

This reality was not in a hurry to turn its sunny side toward the group. The loss of £1.5m following the reduced demand from JCB had delivered such a heavy blow to the Leicester plant that recovery seemed highly unlikely. This foundry, the least specialised one out of the three, also happened to be the one with the least modernised equipment. The chances of finding, any time soon, a new customer whose order could compensate for the massive drop in revenue were slimmer than a catwalk model on a diet. Under these circumstances, keeping the business open and running would have been like forgetting to turn off a kitchen tap: expensive and potentially damaging. So the Board had taken a decision to close down the non-core foundry in Leicester, and in February 2017 it stopped production. All the buildings were flattened down, the contract for lease of the land terminated. The move wasn't quite as dramatic as it might have appeared: all the machinery that was worth rescuing and a number of staff were relocated to the Scunthorpe plant, which had enough space to accommodate the additional facilities and personnel. It also took over Leicester's remaining orders. Maybe it would be fair to say that the Leicester plant didn't fully disappear, but rather was absorbed by, or even evolved into, the Scunthorpe foundry.

Now, just like in the "olden times", at the very beginning of its history, **Chamberlin Plc** had only two iron-melting plants, one of which was the company's very first, original foundry in Walsall. The group had been constantly changing its shape and size by acquiring and losing businesses, and the Chuckery outlasted them all. But this seemingly safe and stable part of **Chamberlin Plc** was also hit by an unexpected problem. Machining, a brand new and potentially highly profitable process that had been incorporated into the foundry's operations only a year before, did not live up to expectations. The equipment, recommended by **BorgWarner**, was not what it seemed to be. As it transpired later, at the time of the installation it had not yet been approved for use in a foundry, and subsequently failed to perform in accordance with the manufacturer's guarantee: in twelve months it processed less than half of the predicted three quarters of a million parts. This inefficiency meant that the underlying operating profit of the foundry decreased from £0.7m to £0.4m. The supplier of the malfunctioning machinery admitted their mistake and agreed to pay **Chamberlin and Hill Castings Ltd** a full compensation which was then used to successfully resolve the technical issues. After the unfortunate "false start" the machining equipment was made fit to deliver the promised results. Chuckery was rapidly filling the so-far vacant niche within the vast and varied automotive market by becoming the only producer of fully machined castings for turbocharger housing, which made up approximately 74% of the total output from Walsall. By the end of the year, **Chamberlin and Hill Castings Ltd** had secured two new major contracts. The chairman's report did not give any details about either of those, but it would be very reasonable to presume that one or even both of them would have involved making castings for the turbocharger housing. From then on, this new "star of the show" was destined to dominate over the production line of Chuckery and, like any true star, was equally capable of being a hero and a villain, a saviour and a destroyer… okay, too many metaphors; I'll stop.

The legacy of the downtime in Chuckery continued to be felt for a long time after the problem with the new equipment had been fixed. Only by the end of 2018, after a full twelve months of contribution from the machining plant, were foundry revenues restored and even increased by 11% to £29.3m. But then the wheel of fortune, again, began to turn the wrong way. In the second part of the following year, sales on the turbocharger market slowed down due to the disruption of the car manufacturers' schedules caused by the new Worldwide Harmonised Light Vehicle Test Procedure (WLTP) emissions testing regime. Additionally, one of the Chuckery's customers fell into administration, reducing the foundry's profit by about £0.1m. From the chairman's report: *"Underlying operating profit in 2019 was below breaking even with a negative margin of -0.7 (2018: +2.0%)."* And all the time, in the background of these financially dramatic events, the pension fund deficit continued to grow, increasing the group's bank overdraft. **Chamberlin Plc** needed to raise a serious sum of money. There were various ways of doing it, but only one way of doing it fast. They needed to sell one of their assets. At the time, the group included four businesses: two foundries in Walsall and Scunthorpe, and two engineering companies, **Petrel** and **Exidor**. The last one on this list had to go.

Looking through the documents, I could not find the justification or even an explanation of that particular choice. If anything, the company producing panic and emergency exit door hardware seemed to be doing really well, and it appears that in 2018 the group had great plans for its development. Here is what the CEO's report said about it: *"Customers place great value on Exidor's heritage as a British designer and manufacturer that delivers high quality, certified products. Its products are for life-critical applications, and it operates in a highly regulated market. We are reengineering the product range to support our growth and continue to target overseas sales while maintaining Exidor's leading position in the UK. The business delivered good growth."* But just a simple line in the next annual report – *"The sale of our Exidor business was a key event in the year"* – summarised the reversal of all those plans as though it was a natural step in the company's progression within the group. Except that "within" actually meant "without".

I asked Gordon to explain to me the directors' decision. Apparently, their reasons were very straightforward. At the time, **Exidor** happened to be simply the most saleable part of the group. German company **ASSA** (whose full name is a little bit longer: **ASSA Abloy Sicherheitstechnik GmbH**), also specialising in all things entrance and exit related, had been interested in **Exidor** for a while, and as soon as it came on the market they were happy to pay £10m. **Chamberlin Plc** used the money, as intended, for the reduction of the pension fund deficit and bank overdraft. As for ex-**Exidor**, it has changed its name and logo, but is very much alive and kicking and, as a subsidiary of **ASSA Abloy**, is still producing first-rate hardware in its factory in Cannock.

Chamberlin Plc was left with only one engineering company. **Petrel** had started off back in the seventies as a manufacturer of electric conduits, then moved on to making high quality lighting and control equipment designed to customers' specifications and intended for use in harsh, unsafe or demanding environments like mines, process plants, offshore platforms or workshops with hazardous conditions. It had an extensive customer base both in the UK and abroad, which was bound to grow further since **Petrel** transitioned to LEDs and broadened the scope of its products to include bespoke lighting for all dark areas as well as a portable light fittings range.

All three divisions of the group seemed to be making steady progress but not without temporary setbacks. The Scunthorpe foundry had developed a serious problem of its own. **Ductile Castings**, a company started by Maurice Love in 1986 and purchased by **Chamberlin and Hill Plc** in 1998, was located on a site adjacent to **British Steel** of Scunthorpe, and up to 50% of **RDC** production was commissioned by its next door neighbour. In the middle of 2019, the latter went out of business. Almost overnight, the Scunthorpe foundry's order book lost half its volume. Redundancies among staff and senior managers followed. The number of workers was dropped to a bare minimum required for retaining all the key skills. Yet this didn't turn out to be a complete disaster: at around the same time, a number of their competitors went bust while **Russell Ductile Castings** remained afloat, though at a severely reduced capacity. Soon enough, the foundry's name and reputation attracted new customers. **Ham Baker Group,** a company that supplied **Thames Tideway** and their "Super Sewer" in London, placed with **RDC** an order for Penstock doors and frames, worth £2m. The capital's sewer system was first built nearly one and a half centuries ago when the population of the city was just over three million people. Today the same structure is still in place and still functioning – but the number of its users has increased threefold. Consequently, every year millions of tonnes of untreated sewage spills into the Thames. To remedy this unsavoury situation, a 25 km long tunnel, known as "Super Sewer", is currently being built under the riverbed in order to intercept the spills and clean up water. With the assistance of penstocks (a type of valve that controls the flow of liquids), the tunnel will protect the river for at least another hundred years – and, probably unbeknownst to Londoners, a contribution from a small foundry in Lincolnshire is helping this happen.

So just like that, by the end of 2019, **Chamberlin Plc**, determined to combine the millennia-old foundry industry and cutting-edge technologies of the twenty-first century, might have discovered its optimal size and composition: two foundries, each with its distinctive "character", and an engineering company with its own place on the global market. The three quite different, individual enterprises shared the ability to adjust to the ever-increasing complexity of modern life. They also shared the management. Talking of which: every one of the companies was run by its own administration coordinated from the group's headquarters in Walsall. The CEO's report explains: *"Each Chamberlin business unit participates in an annual round of planning with the Executive Management, during which performance and future plans for that business are reviewed and updated. These business plans are all aligned with the group business strategy and include specific local and divisional targets and key performance indicators. In addition, individual business reviews take place throughout the year on a regular basis enabling the Board to assess performance."*

These meetings would have taken place at the Walsall foundry, with three men watching over the unfolding events from their portraits on one of the walls of Chuckery's office block: three entrepreneurs that had been there at the very start of what was to become today's collection of companies. I can't help but wonder what would have happened if their photos, like the pictures in the halls of Hogwarts, had suddenly acquired an ability to come to life. These three – James Chamberlin, serious and thoughtful; Henry Hill, smiling good-naturedly into the camera; Herbert Bather, young and quietly self-assured – what would they have said, what would they have felt? Would they have nodded approvingly and given their blessing to their successors or would they have screamed at them in rage, ready to jump out of the frames and demonstrate how things should be done? Was this how they had imagined the remote future of their enterprise?

I am safe posing these questions. With no chance of knowing the real answer, any reply would be as good as the next. So here is mine: I believe that the three men in those portraits had every reason to be proud of what they had created. By 2019, from a single factory in a small-time town somewhere in the middle of the Midlands, after a long 130 years of trading through two world wars and several recessions, through the policies of twenty-seven Prime Ministers and a number of general strikes, through markets crushing and booming again, **Chamberlin and Hill Ltd** grew into an internationally recognised group of companies supplying Great Britain and countries all over the world with various objects needed at any particular time, from tubing connectors used to construct a bed on a submarine in one of the James Bond movies to motor housings for the full range of Vauxhall cars, from door handles to meat grinders, from grenades to griddles. And yes, in recent years the group had faced many challenges, but they kept going and had all that was needed to turn things around.

Then came the year 2020.

Supplement to Part V:
A spa with a difference

Five narrow metal steps take me to the top of what resembles either a small scaffolding or a huge lion cage. I am standing on the grid of the platform, looking around. The view is far from inducing optimistic thoughts. Everywhere – around me and right underneath my feet – is a dense jungle of pipes and slightly ominous looking machinery, all generously sprinkled with some ash-coloured substance, which, come to think of it, might be actual ash. But that's not all. On the concrete floor a couple of metres in front and below the platform sits a vessel filled with softly glistening water-like fluid. "It's caustic soda," says a quiet voice behind me. "You jump in there – nothing is left."

Meet Andy Holden, the ruler of this place. No, not his official job title, but that's what he really is, as superintendent of the C&H finishing department. It's his responsibility to make sure that everything produced here goes out of the foundry's gate in perfect condition: that the turbo inside your car's motor doesn't split right in the middle of a motorway, an insulator in a railway's overhead line doesn't crack, and your favourite cast iron griddle doesn't shatter when you put it on the stove. Today he is showing me around his domain.

"I started in 1979 as a labourer in the finishing department of Bloxwich foundry," he says, *"and went on to become a foreman of the department and then gradually progressed and bettered myself in all the years. By 2005 I was the manager of the core shop. When the Bloxwich foundry closed down, I was transferred to Walsall, and, obviously, they already had supervisors in their*

core shop, but there was a position in the finishing department, and that's where I have been ever since. Now I am a superintendent here."

"Here" is a spacious building, big enough to accommodate, with some room to spare, a few Boeings or similar sized aircraft. From the moment DISA, the mighty moulding machine, spits out a batch of "freshly baked" and still glowing-red castings, they begin their journey around the finishing department. As we walk, following their route, Andy explains:

"When the castings come off the end of DISA we wait for them to cool down a bit, and then they go to the shuffle table where those guys" – he points toward two young men standing at a long bench, armed with hammers – "knock them off the feeders. The castings then go into bins, and the feeders carry on to the end of the shuffle table into a large container and will be sent back to the foundry to be re-melted. Now we shotblast the castings for half an hour to clean them, and then they are ready for the next step: the chemical clean."

I can witness this process because we are standing right over the container filled with the substance capable of dissolving a baby elephant within minutes. Andy sweetly calls it "a bath". (In all fairness, castings are very happy to lie in lye.) Actually, a lot of terms we use in our everyday life do not mean quite the same when used in this place. Where else would you hear the words "bath" and "caustic soda" in the same sentence? Where else does "warming something up" imply bringing its temperature to some 500o C? Then again, "the everyday life" for Andy and his colleagues happens precisely here, within these walls, and the language is a simple reflection of this fact. However, while in the foundry, I would rather keep my distance from any object with a deceptively ordinary name.

After they leave the alkaline spar, castings still have quite a journey ahead before they can be loaded onto a lorry and dispatched to the customer. But that's the story of another department…

HISTORY OF
CHAMBERLIN AND HILL

PART

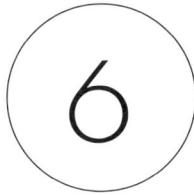

6

31

A near-death experience
(2020)

A bombshell, disguised as an email from the central office for purchasing operations of **BorgWarner**, was dropped on the unsuspecting headquarters of **Chamberlin Plc** on 15th of December 2020. It was followed by a phone call and, soon after, a letter from **BorgWarner's** office in Germany. The message was very clear and yet utterly incomprehensible at the same time: Chuckery's major customer informed the management of the foundry of the termination of all their contracts with effect from 22nd January 2021. Just a quick reminder in order to "set the scene": in 2016, American company **BorgWarner Turbo Systems**, one of the world leaders in the automotive industry, had encouraged the directors of **Chamberlin Plc** to purchase and install a multimillion pound machining plant whose sole purpose was to turn Chuckery's castings into finished turbocharger housings used by **BorgWarner** in their engines. A year later, **Chamberlin Plc** secured a five-year contract for the production of fully machined housings for **BorgWarner**: a massive order that engaged almost the full capacity of the foundry in Walsall. In 2020, two years before the agreement was due to expire, it was abruptly terminated by the automotive giant. *"In hindsight, there had been signs that all was not well. For instance, we had won no new orders from them for a while by then,"* Keith Butler Wheelhouse, the group's Chairman, told me in our brief conversation, *"but no-one could imagine that they would pull out of an existing contract without any warning!"*

That was the incomprehensible part of the message whose echo is still bouncing off the foundry walls even now: I could detect it every time I visited the foundry. It was a weird kind of an echo: instead of the reverberation of sounds that were no longer there, these were waves of silence, the absence of voices that should have been heard. Voices of people made redundant because the jobs they had been doing for years, or even decades, had ceased to exist. People like Dave Marshall, the foreman of the core shop, a man with hands worth their weight in gold who had been telling me about his life while we were looking at the photographs of his incredible artwork on his laptop and who had promised to show me around his department on my next visit – but when I arrived at the foundry the following week, he was no longer there. Voices of some of Chuckery's ex-employees whom I had planned to talk to and failed – not because they were difficult to reach, but because they still felt too bitter to help me record the history of the place to which they had devoted their lives and which had shed them off when the going got tough. And those who have stayed on would never forget that December either. Emotions were running high then. Nobody knew whether they would have a job to return to after the Christmas break. The festive season was flavoured by cloves, cinnamon and anxiety. *"We all were so nervous,"* one of my interviewees told me. *"The uncertainty was unbearable. Suddenly, your plans were in jeopardy."* When asked what their initial thoughts were when they heard the news, he said *"I assumed it was a joke…"* This was an understandable reaction: from a Chuckery worker's point of view, **BorgWarner's** decision simply didn't make any sense and therefore was difficult to believe; soon enough it became clear that this wasn't a laughing matter.

It was hard to imagine a respectable corporation acting like that without a reason. And it had to be a damn good reason – but what exactly was it? I thought that finding an answer to this question was going to be straightforward. I was wrong. And not because one of **Chamberlin's** directors whom I had approached, hoping for an explanation, replied that I "should back off the whole **BorgWarner's** question." No: it transpired that all the reasons, as well as the group's response, and, in fact, the whole **BorgWarner – Chamberlin** relationship, had been covered by a Confidentiality Agreement which, due to its nature, will have to remain, well… confidential. So the document in question cannot be viewed – *dura lex sed lex* – but the political and economic situation, the whole set of circumstances under which the events of 2020 took place are in the open, and anybody is free to examine them and try to figure out what made **BorgWarner** come to that decision.

We tend to take solace in establishing the reason, in discovering the root of our troubles, as if understanding the cause can magically alleviate the consequence. I wonder whether there was a single event that initiated a chain reaction leading to that cold morning in mid-December. If so – what was it? Maybe the very first cough that had started an incessant torrent of disasters which has swept recently over the planet? A new virus spreading, like a forest fire, from city to city, from country to country, from continent to continent, affected everyone in its path – even those who were lucky enough to escape the actual disease. The pandemic descended on us, not only claiming lives, but also destroying relationships, crushing households, ruining businesses. Lockdowns interrupted supply and demand chains. Logistics became problematic. Companies were losing markets and had to adjust to the new reality. And the new reality for the automotive industry could be described in just two words: empty roads. Had this affected **BorgWarner** in such a way that they were no longer capable of producing vehicles at the pre-pandemic rate and consequently – nothing personal, folks! – didn't need the parts made by Chuckery?

Or maybe it was a cross? A simple cross that marked a ballot paper on 23rd of June 2016 and, multiplied by exactly 17,410,742, signified the UK's decision to leave the European Union? Four agonisingly unsettled years followed that fateful date, during which lack of certainty about the new, yet-to-be-established rules of trade made many businesses around the world question the wisdom of continuing a relationship with their British counterparts. One of the features of the "incoming world order" was, however, clear: for the Europeans, the era of tariff-free transactions with the UK was over. **BorgWarner**, although an American company, would have been affected by the increased costs (not to mention the paperwork) that came with the delights of Brexit because their production facility dealing with **Chamberlin** was situated in Germany. Maybe they felt the need to be proactive and, avoiding dependence on their UK partner, started dispersing their orders to China, Korea and Brazil?

I am probably being unreasonable in looking for a single reason here: more likely than not, there would have existed a combination of factors influencing **BorgWarner's** choice and, all of them, at the first glance, outside of **Chamberlin's** control ("at the first glance" being a key phrase here). The solid fact is this: the group was in trouble. The production of turbocharger housings still continued a few months past the deadline set in the email, but the prospects of quickly finding a replacement for **BorgWarner's** orders were non-existent. The Walsall foundry went from functioning to its full capacity to not having enough work for so much as breaking even. The machining plant became obsolete. With Chuckery out of action, the financial hole at the edge of which **Chamberlin Plc** had been balancing for a while by then, was about to swallow the group without a trace. **RDC** and **Petrel**, even though they were profitable, would not have been an anchor strong enough to stop the fall. For the first time in its history, the very existence of the group was under threat.

The compensation received from **BorgWarner** for terminating the contract early – £300,000 – didn't even come close to covering **Chamberlin's** losses. Urgent and desperate measures were taken in order to rescue the situation. Jobs were cut, the numbers of senior management reduced. The very expensive and now utterly useless machining plant was put up for sale but no buyer was found.

The situation remained dire.

Not that all those measures were ineffective. They were simply insufficient. Under different circumstances they might have helped, but in 2020, attempts to rescue the situation by some redundancies and a bit of restructuring were an equivalent to trying to put out a forest fire with a watering can. Something a little stronger was required: perhaps they needed a knight in shining armour storming, astride a white horse, out of some fairy tale straight into the group's troubled headquarters.

32

Alpine views
(2021)

The evident absence of fairy tales in our reality didn't automatically exclude such a possibility. And so it happened. Except that a modern day knight took the form of a wealthy entrepreneur, his shining armour reincarnated into a (far better suited for the purpose) track record of successful investments, and a white horse was replaced by a more efficient black Mercedes (very likely powered by a motor with a turbocharger housing cast by Chuckery, but this would have been just a coincidence). Here is how the CEO's report announced that event: "*In March 2021, the Board was strengthened by the appointment of Trevor Brown, initially as a Non-Executive Director, and in June 2021 as an Executive Director with the responsibility for strategy. Trevor brings a wealth of entrepreneurial experience to the board, which will be invaluable as we embark upon a new strategy for growth.*" I should add here that it was a wealth not only of his entrepreneurial experience that he contributed to the group. As if by magic, Trevor Brown, an enigmatic "accidental CEO" as he was once called, appeared on the scene just when that scene was about to collapse. What might have looked like an act of serendipity happened to be a thoroughly calculated and immaculately timed event, as I found out when I made an attempt to decode the enigma and demystify the magic. To do that, I had to relocate (just for a couple of hours and, sadly, only virtually) from not-so-sunny Birmingham to often-excessively-sunny Zug, a small town in the Swiss Alps where my interviewee, a native Londoner, had been living for the past fifteen years.

Until very recently, a simple Google search would have revealed Trevor Brown's impressive portfolio of investments and senior managerial positions in a number of companies, such as **Braveheart Investment Group Plc, Remote Monitoring Systems, Management Resource Solutions** to name just a few. As diverse as these businesses appeared to be, they nevertheless had one thing in common: all of them were involved in scientific research with commercial applications. In 2021, **Chamberlin Plc** was added to that list: a company that could not have been more different from the rest. I simply had to ask why. From his Alpine retreat, Trevor replied:

"My history in the past 12 years has been associated with companies developing sophisticated technologies and producing submicroscopic things: intellectual, rather than physical, artefacts. This reflected a personal interest of mine – and yet, at the same time I longed for something more tangible. As a child, I lived near a railway track of the London – Midlands line. I was fascinated by steam engines. I remember standing early in the morning somewhere like Kings Cross, and there would be several trains there, puffing, ready to go – I loved it! There was something about Chamberlin that fed into that feeling: molten iron, smoke and steam – this really primal, basic stuff. And best of all, at the end of the production line there was a product that I couldn't just put into my pocket or into an envelope like a memory stick: it was tangible, simple, down-to-Earth and immensely satisfying."

I asked, *"Was a wish to tap into a childhood memory really so strong that it alone forced you out of your comfort zone?"*

He replied, *"By the time I got involved with Chamberlin I'd managed a number of businesses which made me realise that there were things that I could do, things that I was good at. But at some point one's comfort zone begins to feel too tight and becomes uncomfortable. So I started looking for a new challenge, and I loved the straightforward nature of Chamberlin's enterprise: at the beginning of the process there was a pile of raw, meaningless stuff, and at the end of it appeared a perfectly formed and purposeful object. It felt like reversing entropy, like making something out of nothing… I approached the Group, and eventually they 'let me in'. This was the case of my track record speaking in my favour."*

Here I would like to add that Trevor Brown's track record, apart from being imposing, had another interesting quality: until 2010, it had been simply non-existent as far as the City was concerned. But around that time, he was appointed a director of Care Capital. It has cascaded from there. Trevor's name started appearing on boards of various companies, culminating in 2015 when he made the headlines becoming a CEO of a well-known investment group and soon after turning it from loss-making to profitable. But the longer we talked, the more I realised that this particular "accident", as well as all the other "chance events" in his life had very little to do with some elusive chance. They organically followed from his ability to recognise an opportunity the moment it presented itself, and his willingness and stamina to act on it. The story of his life before this point in time would be more fitting for an adventure movie than for a book on the history of a business. So here it is compressed into a sentence: born into a poverty-stricken family, spending a large part of his childhood on hospital wards, immobilised in bed in order to stop TB from destroying his bones and, having missed most of his formal education, he nevertheless got an MBA, hitchhiked around the world, started (from zero) and successfully managed a number of businesses, has worked for government, and, eventually, became interested in **Chamberlin Plc**.

When I asked why he wasn't "let in" straight away, and what happened after his first attempt, Trevor replied *"I had been watching the Group for a while by then and initially approached them well before the pandemic. Being an objective outsider, I could spot the mistakes they were making or were about to make. But being on the inside, they didn't see what I saw. I tried to buy shares – unsuccessfully. I had to sit and watch the company being mismanaged into the ground. The situation continued to get from bad to worse and, several months later, in 2021, I simply picked up a phone and tried again. And this time it worked, due to the combination of their position, which was desperate, and my track record that I mentioned earlier. I made my offer, we haggled and came to an agreement. I put in some cash to stop the company from going into administration and then organised and led a fundraising. I invested £1.5 million, and we raised another £3.5million. It was a good first step on the way to recovery."*

I noted, *"Your MBA thesis was about positive aspects of a niche enterprise. You must be in favour of this kind of business model, and you have successfully applied it in practice. How do you square your conviction with the fact that it was precisely being in a niche that nearly killed **Chamberlin plc**?"*

"First of all, they did not occupy a niche," he replied *"Not really. The main point about a niche is that you can control it. You need domination.*

Chamberlin didn't have that. The product they were making, the turbocharger housings, apparently was not as unique as they presumed it to be. It could have been sourced, as evidence subsequently showed, somewhere else in the world. **BorgWarner** didn't stop buying castings from **Chamberlin** because they no longer needed those castings. They simply transferred their business to other places. It is always a mistake to rely on one customer, however convenient this might seem. Circumstances change, companies go bust, contracts get terminated. One hopes that nothing of the kind would happen, but it does. Optimism kills more businesses than pessimism."

Trevor carried on methodically, bit by bit, explaining at what point and in what way mistakes had been made. I suddenly felt the ground crumbling beneath my feet, as if this conversation were taking place without the assistance of the Internet, as if I were actually there, balancing high above sea level somewhere in the Alps, right on the edge of a cliff, dislodging debris into the void. The picture of the universe (or rather of one of its fragments) that I had carefully created in my mind was no longer true. All – or almost all – that I thought I had understood about the recent events affecting **Chamberlin Plc** happened to be wrong: the group hadn't simply fallen prey to some unforeseen and unfortunate circumstances completely outside of anyone's control. No. Mistakes that had been made could not be explained by anything other than managerial incompetence and failure to think a few steps ahead. Profitable, successful and thriving **Exidor**, the "golden goose" of the group, had been sold in all but name, to be replaced by the machining equipment designed to handle one specific type of product and to serve the needs of a single customer on a five-year contract. If there was some hidden wisdom in this decision, it was hidden too well to be seen. As for the contract itself, it's hard to imagine that a carefully thought through, professionally drafted legal document would have been so easy to breach with so little inconvenience for the "breaching party". I had to urgently reconstruct my "worldview"; its new, updated version turned out to be less rose-tinted but sharper and more satisfying because it included some clearly defined routes out of the cul-de-sac, both in the short and in the long run. Meanwhile, our conversation continued. Trevor said: "The pandemic – or anything else external – was not fully to blame for all the problems. The 'key wrong decision' had been made a while back. Investing millions of pounds into the machining plant was a catastrophe waiting to happen."

"If it were possible," I wondered, *"some time in the future, to find a way of operating the machining plant as intended – would it solve all the problems of the Group?"*

"No," he said, *"The central problem of the casting business is capacity. When you reach the point where you can't produce any more... you can't produce any more! What do you do then? Extend the premises? Nowadays, just the planning application for a foundry would take some ten years to get."*

"So the company is doomed, then?"

"No, not at all. There are ways of revitalising the business. Maybe this has happened for a reason. The time of trouble is a perfect time to shake things up, to think outside the box. Never waste a good crisis!"

And it seems they didn't. They used it to examine their past mistakes and adjust present strategies in order to guarantee future success. A decent "chunk" of the capital they needed to raise had been hidden in plain sight all this time, and the current crisis made it clearly visible: the grounds of Scunthorpe foundry. This extensive – and expensive! – piece of land belonged to the group, so the foundry was almost literally standing on a pile of cash. The solution was right there: sell the plot and rent it back from the buyer since the cost of the lease would pale into insignificance compared to the income from the sale. From this transaction the group received one and a quarter million pounds; some of the money went into the pension fund and some was used to increase the working capital.

To prevent a repetition of the disaster with **BorgWarner** and to make the Walsall foundry immune to its dependency on one customer, the group has changed its basic policy that determined the range and the quantity of products to be manufactured. This new approach was stated in the CEO's report: *"The Board's aim in the medium term is to replace the majority of the Group's traditional, low-margin contract-based production with much higher margin, premium consumer products."* This simply meant that, instead of – or maybe in addition to – relying on the demands of the automotive industry and manufacturing castings with complex internal structure, they needed to start making something entirely different, maybe less labour intensive but more cost effective, and selling it directly to the "end-users" of that product.

33

Foundries Are Go!
(2022)

The pandemic, regardless of whether or not it had been partially responsible for the foundry's recent misfortune, definitely helped to find a way out of the crisis. The very first lockdown that brought the whole country to a standstill in March 2020 didn't simply reshape people's way of life. It also changed their attitudes and swapped around their priorities. Everybody, apart from the frontline workers and Downing Street party attendees, found themselves trapped in their own homes with too much time, in addition to sanitising gel, on their hands. Everyone reacted differently to such an unprecedented situation. Some headed straight to their sofas. Others ran to the nearest park. Some put Domino's on speed dial. Others dusted off their Nigellas and Olivers. It was the latter category of people for whom Chuckery developed both its brand new ranges, IFW and Emba.

Carl Darby, the IT and E-commerce Director of **Chamberlin Plc**, explained to me how they had made the choice of those additions to the foundry's "repertoire":

> "As soon as we recovered from the shock of the first lockdown, we began our research, studying the market and looking for cast iron products we could manufacture here in Walsall. We discovered that, at the time, the most sought-after thing was gym equipment. All the fitness centres were shut. People who were used to exercising had to do it at home. For that, they needed their tools. But supply

then was very low. It couldn't keep up with the demand. So in September 2020 we came up with an idea of IFW (Iron Foundry weights), started the production, and already in November our kettlebells went on sale."

The success of the new range offered on Amazon and **Chamberlin Plc's** own website exceeded everybody's expectations. (Here, sticking to the innate rules of storytelling, I was supposed to back up the previous statement by providing the number of items sold, but apparently these figures fall under the category of "sensitive information" and are not to be disclosed.) At first, this "collection" consisted of just one type of kettlebell varying in weight from four to twenty-four kilograms. Then, in March 2021, a natural follow-up product, the weight plate, was added to the range. Deep dish plates, renowned for their functionality and a vintage appearance, and dumbbells are now in the pipeline.

I looked up the IFW products: on Amazon the kettlebells had remarkable ratings 4.7 and 4.8 (out of 5) stars, and as a frequent visitor of this online retailer I can assert that not many goods receive such a high recognition here… and yet I was not convinced. I had absolutely no reason not to believe all the positive reviews, and the weights really did look stunning: polished, smooth and shiny – but I still needed to understand why one would choose this type of kettlebell over a cheaper (indisputable fact) and prettier (my subjective opinion) version of the same thing coated in soft-ish looking, cheerfully coloured neoprene. So I walked into a gym on my local High Street and ambushed an unsuspecting fitness instructor with the physique of someone who, unlike me, had seen these kettlebells on a regular basis and not just in a photo. I asked him whether the monochrome solid-iron weights had any advantages over their flamboyant plastic-clad alternatives. The fitness pro, whom I had appointed to be my expert in the matter, answered without any hesitation or deviation:

"have three kettlebells at home, one solid iron and two covered in some sort of synthetic, all bought at roughly the same time. The only one that looks brand new is the cast iron one. The other two show some wear and tear, they mark easily. The solid iron gets a bit hot in the summer when used outside, but other than that I can't find any fault in it. If I were to choose another kettlebell now I would definitely go for a cast iron one."

Four hundred yards further, and another guy at another fitness centre was even more categorical in his opinion:

> *"We would never use anything other than cast iron weights in this gym. All the fancy looking kettlebells and plates are not accurate enough. Only the cast iron ones are. We have many professional bodybuilders training here. They know their stuff. And they never touch anything that's not solid iron."*

Not only our fitness regimes have been affected by the lockdowns. The way we cook has also changed – and who knows? – maybe forever. It was one of those rare cases when two wrongs made a right. The trend of the 1970s that had seen people abandoning traditional methods of cooking in favour of pre-prepared microwavable meals of questionable nutritional value was swiftly reversed by the pandemic. Our lives in lockdowns were described by a simple formula: free time plus health concerns minus access to catering facilities equals increased interest in applied gastronomy. And the market reflected this new development. Here is Carl Darby again:

> *"Our research showed that the next most popular product behind gym equipment was actually cookware. And further research revealed a specific gap in the UK market. There was an unsatisfied demand for high quality, premium cast iron products. So we made a move to fill the gap. In February 2021, we developed our brand new range Emba."*

This new range that went on sale in November 2021 consisted of griddles and ten inch skillets. "Emba", being a sensational spelling of "ember", is meant to remind the potential buyers of the fiery manner in which these items are produced. The pans themselves, regardless of the orthographic frivolities in the brand's name, have been manufactured with the strictest adherence to all the possible rules. Every item of the range has been pre-seasoned to ensure a hassle-free non-stick finish, and every single one of them can be used on the hob, in the oven, on a BBQ or even on open fire, making Emba skillets and griddles some of the most versatile on the market. But this versatility and practicality (qualities applicable to IFW as well) are not the only features that lift these brands into the premium category. Both ranges have been designed and manufactured in the UK from recycled iron, so anybody worrying about the health of the planet as well as their own can use these with a clear conscience. High durability and performance of the products are guaranteed by Chuckery's craftsmanship: of all the problems that this foundry has experienced in its (very long) time of trading, not a single one has ever been caused by substandard quality of its castings.

It appears that my story – and **Chamberlin's** history – has finally moved from the past into the present. It's time to look around instead of looking back. And this is what I see: both foundries seem to be on the way to overcoming the problems of the recent and not-so-recent past. **RDC** has been profitable since the collapse of **British Steel** in 2019. Their £3.5m order book is now fuller than ever. **Chamberlin and Hill Ltd**, aka Chuckery, having moved along a not entirely obstacle-free path, completed the circle and rediscovered its original mission that had made it so successful at the very beginning of its existence: production of high quality household goods. But will the clever sliding doors beneath the Thames be able to prevent the group from sinking? Will the perfectly formed kettlebells be heavy enough to add sufficient positive momentum to the whole enterprise? Secretly hoping to hear a cheerful "yes", I asked some of my trusty consultants whether the progress made by Chuckery and **RDC** could become the very force that would propel **Chamberlin Plc** into the future – and my hopes for a "happy ever after" of the foundries (and a happy ending of the book) were dampened.

The world in which James Chamberlin and Henry Hill opened their first foundry was very different from the one in which we live now. That world was not only 132 years younger, it was bigger – even if not in the actual physical size. Decades before the globe turned into a global marketplace, companies serving the same industry were situated, largely, within one country and traded under identical conditions. To succeed, one needed to be just that little bit savvier, just a tad more enterprising and, possibly, just a dash more lucky than one's competitors. Evidently, both founders of **Chamberlin and Hill Ltd** had all the qualities required for achieving their goals. At the time when they were putting their skills into practice, a large, densely populated country on the other side of the continent, crushed and humiliated by several wars it had been involved in, was struggling to survive and could not even dream of becoming, one day in the not-so-near future, a state as powerful as we know it now. Since then, "the rules of engagement" have changed. Today **Chamberlin's** foundries have to compete not only with British and European businesses, but also with China, the world leader in price undercutting: this, just like attempting to win a marathon against someone who is whizzing past you on a motorbike, is patently a pointless pursuit. Being a foundry version of Primark while producing vast quantities of low-margin "mass market" items (a strategy that had worked well in the past) is no longer a viable option: somewhere in the depths of the Celestial Empire there always will be a company capable of delivering the same volumes of seemingly the same castings for a fraction of the price, no matter how low that price already was! Instead, one could choose to go the "haute couture" route (or should it be "haut fondre"?) and become a "designer" manufacturer targeting a selected group of consumers. The "Emba" range – unique, sophisticated, good looking and durable – fits perfectly with Chuckery's new image of iron smelting "boutique". **RDC**, with the highly specialised orders it has been recently attracting, is also an example of this mode of trading: the mode that will enable both companies to thrive.

Yet, considering the specifics of the modern market, the foundries' success is a necessary but not a sufficient condition for guaranteeing the group's return to its former glory. A better potential for substantial profits, fewer competitors and an unrestricted capacity for growth are required to give the enterprise a chance to "live long and prosper", and, luckily, one of **Chamberlin's** divisions might just be able to tick all the right boxes...

34

Time to meet Cinderella
of Chamberlin
(2022, continued)

t has been present in this story since 1982, when **Solenoids and Regulators Ltd** absorbed a range of flameproof appliances from **Conduit Fittings Ltd** resulting, eventually, in the creation of **Petrel Ltd**. The new company was named for a bird that spends most of its life flying over the sea, often being the only creature observed from the oil rigs which have always been at the top of **Petrel's** potential client list: a nice change from the more prosaic names of other **Chamberlin** subsidiaries. Initially, the company was situated in the Aston area of Birmingham, but moved to larger premises in a suburban village of Marston Green near Solihull in 1997. A member of the group for the past forty years, it hasn't been the focus of the CEO's reports, appearing to blend into the background. With all the attention concentrated on its "older sisters", the foundries, **Petrel**, producing a variety of safety lights intended for use in dangerous environments, seemed to be a "Cinderella of Chamberlin": low-key, hardworking and reliable. And, like any true Cinderella, this company was destined one day to come out of the shadows.

The idea of diversification of the group's business interests isn't new. As far back as the mid-1970s, **Chamberlin Plc** (actually, still **Chamberlin and Hill Ltd** back then) started to shift the emphasis from iron smelting to electrical and mechanical technology by purchasing engineering companies. Whether they foresaw the future developments in the foundry industry, or simply followed the folk wisdom advising not to put all the eggs in one basket, remains unclear. But they were right regardless of their motives: it looks like the millennia-old trade is about "to go through the change". Iron, the "key ingredient" of the industry, is facing competition from other materials, and the conventional process of casting metal might soon be replaced – at least, when producing smaller items – by a much more sophisticated, cost-effective and precise 3D laser printing. **Petrel**, on the other hand, has all the features of a future-proof company combining the latest, environmentally friendly technology with high adaptability. So what do the premises of the business advertising itself as "*an established UK manufacturer of high-performance LED and fluorescent lighting solutions for use in harsh and hazardous areas providing a wide range of fixed and portable lighting for sale and hire*" look like?

About a year after my first visit to the Walsall foundry, I went to the factory in Marston Green. Clare Hipkiss, the company's Operations Director, had just returned from her summer break but managed to find a bit of time to show me around. In stark contrast to the overwhelmingly dramatic atmosphere of Chuckery, **Petrel's** manufacturing site looked and felt almost serene: it was a vast space saturated with light (daylight for that matter, not the variety that flows out of the devices made here), and filled with specialised equipment including power presses, CNC (computer numerical control) machines, paint spray plant, assembly lines and testing appliances. The space was divided into self-contained "isles" of different sizes: in each of these a specific product can be made from start to finish. No need for earplugs here: not that this place was totally quiet, but the noise coming from some of the isles (knocking and high pitched dental-drill-like whir) was nowhere near as intense as the audio background of the foundry. Before I could share that observation with Clare, a roaring sound penetrated the roof of the building, getting louder and louder but mercifully disappearing just seconds later: the plant is situated within the control zone for Birmingham International, and so it feels as if any plane taking off or preparing for landing flies directly (and not very high) above the ceiling. Clare laughed: "*It used to be a lot worse some years ago!*"

We walked between the little bays where the future lights were being made. The "new-borns" lying there didn't appear to be anything special: minimalistic designs, utilitarian shapes; only the colour of their bodies, the "signature colour" of **Petrel** – teal-green, bright, optimistic and decorative – would stop one from labelling them "boring-looking". Then again, looks are not in the "job description" of these devices whose purpose is to provide reliable and totally risk-free illumination in industrial settings where the ordinary lighting fixtures could easily cause fire or explosion.

> *"When I mention 'hazardous zones' people immediately think of gas and oil rigs," said Clare, "but those are just a few examples of such areas and, in fact, we don't supply that many of them. There are plenty more places that are considered hazardous. A flammable substance filling the air: gas (like alcohol or petrol vapours) or small solid particles (like dust or fibres) is potentially explosive or combustible and should not be exposed to a source of ignition. So our lights are indispensable in distilleries, chemical processing plants, car garages, dry cleaning facilities, spray paint booths, wood processing workshops, grain stores, even chocolate making factories – the full list is too long…"*

The lights manufactured by **Petrel** contain a captive diffuser (compacted glass beads and resin closures) with an isolation switch – this excludes the possibility of a spark escaping the device – and they go through a battery of rigorous tests to prove their safety. These tests are conducted offsite, by a company called **Certification Management Ltd,** where **Petrel's** products are subjected to a "trial by ordeal", twenty-first century style: they have to demonstrate their ability to function safely and reliably while being exposed to wet and explosive environments like mist or combustible dust. And they pass with flying colours! Certified to internationally recognised standards, these lights attract customers from all around the world. And the world, by now seriously and not unreasonably concerned with its own wellbeing, has been asking its inhabitants for a little TLC – so moving toward more efficient electrical appliances has become one of the most urgent priorities in developed countries. The UK government has decided to phase out the sale of fluorescent tubes and lamps from September 2023, and **Petrel** is right on target by adjusting its production lines accordingly. All the devices of different shapes and in various stages of their completeness that I saw during the tour around the factory were equipped with LEDs. Clare lifted one of the lights: a square box, with rounded corners, looking a bit like a small old-fashioned portable TV set whose "screen" was studded with rows of tiny pale yellow dots.

"We are making these now," she said. *"They use half the energy of the fluorescent ones. And you don't need to change the tube every eight months or so. LEDs will last almost forever. We've won several contracts to supply large ships like Queen Mary. A batch is about to go to Queen Elizabeth as well. These are portable lights, they can be carried anywhere around the ship. What's so special about them is that the LEDs get encapsulated, covered by a transparent rock-hard encapsulant, so, if overheated, the circuit will simply cut out, and no spark can possibly escape."*

We walked further, and at one of the workstations I noticed a pile of yellow-bodied lights which looked out of place in the sea of "petrel-green". I was surprised: by then I knew that the colour was an important part of the **Petrel** brand. This particular shade had been chosen decades ago by John Bather who had seemed to have a soft spot for green, so much so that during his "time in office" the company's old logo and all the woodwork in the buildings belonging to C&H were painted that colour. Since then, the doors and skirting boards have given in to the demands of ever-changing decor-fashion, but **Petrel's** products have remained true to the tradition. Clare explained:

"One of our competitors came to us and said, 'your lights are better than ours, can you make some but put our logo on them?' We said 'of course we can!' – and this is what those yellow ones are. So not only we got rid of a competitor but also gained extra orders! Adjusting the colour wasn't a problem: we have our own spray station."

"Would you be able to customise any characteristics of your lights other than the colour?" I asked.

"Yes, we can adjust our designs as long as it's not impacting the safety of the product. For example, we had a request from our customer, a distillery up North, asked for a more pleasant lighting for their 'whiskey tour'. They wanted the barrels to be softly illuminated to make it a better experience for their visitors. So we've put some orange film over the LEDs to achieve that warm gentle glow."

"How do you sell your products?"

"We use distributors and wholesalers but also sell directly to customers; we've got a number of regulars such as Dragon LNG, a terminal for liquefied natural gas based in Pembrokeshire. They receive liquid gas shipped from around the world and re-gasify it, turning it back to its natural state. Considering the highly combustible environment of the terminal, the specialised electrical equipment is a necessity there. They used to order our lights and then decided to try out other suppliers. So they did. And after that they came back to us. Which is not surprising: our products really are the best of their kind that you can buy on the market today. They are exceptionally safe and efficient: with our lights you get such a great output that you would only need one of them, while with other companies' lights you'd have to put two together side-by-side to achieve the same effect!"

Our voices, again, were drowned by the noise of a plane flying right over our heads. I knew it was not very likely, but couldn't help thinking: was this particular one heading to Scotland carrying, among other things, **Petrel's** lights to the **InchDairnie Distillery** for its whiskey tours: those warm-orange-tinted safety lights designed to allow angels to have their share completely risk-free?

35

Instead of an epilogue…

In the past several years, we have developed a sincere, well-deserved and long overdue interest in the sources of our food. Everything that sits on a spoon before going into one's mouth has suddenly become a matter of utmost importance, if not an obsession. But what about the spoon itself? Does anybody ever care about the origins of everyday objects as useful but mundane as that? I certainly did not.

Until just over a year ago.

Just over a year ago, for the first time in my life, I walked into a place about which I knew only one thing: that it existed. The word "foundry" meant as much to me as the word "deoxyribonucleic" does to a preschooler. A lot has changed since then. All my preconceptions, my views, my attitude toward anything industry-related have melted away like snow after a freak late-March snowfall. A year spent visiting arguably one of the most gripping and dramatic man-made places on Earth, a foundry, and talking to people who work or used to work there has made me realise that there is nothing ordinary about "ordinary" objects. Every single one of those, at first glance commonplace, "boring" things is hiding a story as exciting as stories behind the most revered pieces of art. I will never be able to look again at a standard frying pan, be it produced by Chamberlin or some other company, without thinking of all the human ingenuity, immense mental and physical efforts and entrepreneurial prowess that are embedded into it.

I am grateful to all the amazing people from Chuckery and Petrel who have assisted me in this journey: the "wise man of Chamberlin" Gordon Stanley, my guide through the "circles of Chuckery" who knows all that there is to know about the group and more; retired foundry man Michael Povey, who has tackled all life's challenges with the quiet dignity of a stoic; ex-coreshop manager David Marshall, whose incredible drawing skills would turn a professional artist green with envy; Trade Union veteran, self-described as "a fighter for the little man", Derek Geoffrey Rudd, Bloxwich's very own Santa who buys Christmas presents for all the kids on his street with his presumably not-such-a-bountiful pension; Walsall foundry's superintendent Peter Singh who doesn't believe in the impossible, accepts any challenge as a dare and takes it on just for the fun of it; Chuckery's Technical Manager Rob Heyworth, a creative guy who designs the foundry's new products in very rare spare moments while doing his main job; Planning and Logistics manager Andy Clark, who divides his time between a computer desk and the shop floor making sure that there is a constant flow of processed orders – and many, many others, those who are mentioned in the book and those who are not. I will remember every single one of them.

And just one more thing: having examined 132 years of the group's history, I have developed an "educated gut feeling" that, provided humanity does not re-enact the story of Atlantis on a planetary scale, **Chamberlin Plc**, formerly **Chamberlin and Hill Ltd**, will still be here in the next 130. It might be composed of different companies; its headquarters might move from Walsall to Birmingham, Leicester or Mars – but it will still be here, and, finely tuned in to the demands of time, it will continue manufacturing its extraordinary ordinary objects… So I would love it if I could "pass the baton" to a future researcher who might decide to write up the next chapter of the **History of Chamberlin and Hill**.

Supplement for Part VI:
Cast of Directors in Order of Appearance

Chamberlin & Hill Ltd (Public Company on the Birmingham Stock Exchange)

George A L Hatton
Chairman 1945 – 1959

George Arthur Lyon Hatton (1888 – 1959) was born in his ancestral home, Hagley Hall. A solicitor by profession, he served as a senior partner in the Birmingham firm of solicitors, Sydney Mitchell and Chattock. As an army captain, he fought in World War One in the Queen's Own (Royal West Kent Regiment); was held as a prisoner-of-war in both Germany and Holland. He was a President of the committee of the Birmingham Law Society in 1950/5.

S H Hinde
Managing Director 1945 – 1949

Sydney Herbert Hinde was born in Rushall, Walsall, in 1890. In his early years, he was a General Manager in a malleable iron foundry which made him perfectly qualified to take a leading role in C&H.

C M Bather:
Director 1945 – 1971

Christina Millar Bather, a qualified state registered physio-therapist, after the death of her husband Herbert Fiennes Bather took a position on the board. She ensured that the company's employees had excellent working conditions.

E H Page:
Company Secretary 1939 – 1966
General Manager/Secretary 1950 – 1951
Commercial Manager/Secretary 1952 – 1954
Director 1954 – 1968
Finance Director 1968 – 1972
Commercial Director 1972 – 1976
Export Director 1976 – 1978

A man of many talents ,Edward Harold Page joined the company in 1939 and contributed greatly to its growth.

P W Adshead

Managing Director 1950 – 1954

Prior to his appointment at C&H, Col. Percy Willets Adshead, formerly Accountant-General of Nigeria, served in the Royal Regiment of Artillery during the First World War.

M M Hallett

Managing Director 1954 – 1976
Non-Executive Director 1976 – 1979

Michael Mountjoy Hallett, Fellow of the Institute of Metallurgists, was president of the Institute of British Foundrymen and president of the International Institute of Foundrymen. In 1971, he was awarded a CBE for services to the iron founding industry.

Sir F Scopes

Chairman 1960 – 1971

Sir Frederick Scopes was Managing Director of The Stanton Iron Works and a director of several other companies. He was a prolific writer of reference books for the iron industry, some still for sale on Amazon.

H P Taylor

Local Director 1962 – 1966
Technical Director 1966 – 1971

Harry Philpotts Taylor had joined C&H in 1940 as a manager at the Lichfield works. He assisted Mr S Hinde during the reconstruction of the new Lichfield foundry. Harry was a local Lichfield councillor, Sheriff of Lichfield, and in 1956 Lord Mayor of Lichfield Council.

T Shaw

Local Director 1962 – 1963

Before becoming a director, Thomas (Tom) Shaw had held the position of works manager at the Walsall foundry for twenty-two years. Unfortunately, he was taken ill soon after his appointment. A keen cricketer, he used to play as a wicket keeper for Walsall Cricket Club.

J K Bather

Local Director 1962 – 1966
Production Director 1969 – 1975
Dep. Managing Director 1975 – 1976
Group Managing Director 1976 – 1995
Non-Exec. Deputy Chair 1995 – 1997

Sir John Knollys Bather was the third generation of the Bather family at C&H, having joined the company in 1961. He was Lord Lieutenant of Derbyshire in 1994 – 2009 and was knighted in his final year.

K B Walton

Director 1970 – 1976
Dep. Managing Director 1976 – 1997

Kenneth Bert Walton (Ken) came into the company as a consultant working for W E Harrison & Co, Management Consultants. He was in charge of installing a system quantifying the manufacturing costs of individual castings. Ken had served in the RAF and played tennis to a good level. After his retirement, he devoted some of his free time to Walsall Central Hall Methodist Church working with the youth of Walsall.

F Grant

Company Secretary 1968 – 1987

Fred Grant joined C&H in 1946 and oversaw the administration of the Walsall Office. Later he took the position of Assistant Company Secretary and, following Harold Page's promotion to Finance Director, became Company Secretary. A lover of classical music, Fred was the Chairman of the Wolverhampton Recorded Music Society.

P E H Bell

Company Secretary 1987 – 1995
Finance Director and Secretary 1995 – 2004

Peter Edwin Helmut Bell had joined C&H straight after school, sponsored by the company. He gained his qualifications in management accountancy and became a member of the Chartered Institute of Secretaries. Initially Peter worked closely with Fred Grant; he became Group Accountant under the guidance of Ken Walton.

T Martin

Deputy Chairman 1970 – 1971
Chairman 1971 – 1980

Tom Martin's wide knowledge of C&H prior to joining the board came from his time as a board member of PA Management Consultants.

F K Howlett

Local Director 1970 – 1985
Group Technical Director - 1985

Fred Kirkby Howlett started working at C&H as a manager at Lichfield foundry. During his term, Lichfield contributed a good share of profit to the group's continued expansion. Towards the end of his career, Fred, like his predecessor, was promoted to Group Technical Director.

P P Ralph

Non-Executive Director 1972 – 1997

Philip Pyman Ralph, a quiet and sharp-minded man, was a merchant banker, a Director of Hill Samuel Ltd., and joint Managing Director of Spey Investments Ltd. During his time at C&H, the company's chairmen sought and respected his views on the running of the business.

N B Williams

Group Production Director 1976 – 1995
Chief Executive Officer 1995 – 2006

Norman Barrie Williams (Barrie) had started his employment at C&H as a metallurgist, but it soon became apparent to Michael Hallett and the board that he could be a useful addition to the management and later to the boardroom.

J R Eades

Non- Executive Director 1978 – 1979
Chairman 1980 – 1982

Before taking his position at C&H, John Robert Eades had been a CEO of Allied Breweries, a director of Huntley and Palmers, London and Midland Steel Scaffolding. Unfortunately, he was tragically incapacitated following a fall and died four months later.

A R Edwards
Group Director 1984 – 2001

Alfred Raymond Edwards was a Managing Director of Petrel Ltd and a main board Director. He supervised the factory's relocation and managed to expand their customer base despite the depressed activity in the oil-related industries.

J D Eccles
Chairman 1983 – 2004

In 1985, John Dawson Eccles, Viscount, was awarded a CBE; on the 24th of February 1999, he inherited the hereditary peerage from his father, The Right Honourable David McAdam Eccles, 1st Viscount Eccles. He was General Manager and Chief Executive of the Commonwealth Development Corporation and has served on the board of many companies.

N C D Kuenssberg
Non- Executive Director 2000 – 2006

Nicholas Christopher Dwelly Kuenssberg, Honorary Professor of University of Glasgow and visiting professor of Strathclyde University, has been a director of Standard Life, Scottish Power and many other companies as well as holding positions of Deputy Chair of the Scottish Environment Protection Agency, Chair of Glasgow School of Art, and QAA Scotland. He is one of Scotland's most distinguished and influential business leaders and is fluent in French, German, Spanish and Italian.

A Vicary
Director & Managing Director, C&H Castings
2001 – 2010

As a university graduate, Adam Vicary joined C&H in September 1988. Ten years later, he became a Managing Director of Ductile Castings and in 2001 joined the board, having responsibility for all foundry operations.

T H P Brown

Non – Executive Chairman 2003 – 2012

Before joining C&H, Thomas Henry Phelps Brown had been a Group Managing Director of Fenner Plc (a major customer of Lichfield foundry) and Group Chief Executive of United Industries.

S C Duckworth

Finance Director 2004 – 2006

Prior to his appointment at C&H, a chartered accountant Simon Charles Duckworth was a Finance Director at Compass Software Group Plc. He had also worked with Price Waterhouse.

F K J Jackson

Non – Executive Director 2005 – 2019

Before joining C&H, Francis Keith John Jackson was a director of many companies and pension funds, including Tarmac Plc and Cape Plc. He was also a senior independent director and chairman of the Audit Committee.

Chamberlin Plc

T M Hair

Chief Executive Officer 2006 – 2013

Timothy Melville Hair was previously Managing Director of Sterling Hydraulics, and his career includes senior positions in a range of engineering businesses.

M J T Bache

Finance Director 2006 – 2012

Mark John Thomas Bache was previously Finance Director of PEL Group Ltd; he has held senior financial positions in several manufacturing groups since qualifying as a Chartered Accountant with PWC in 1988.

A Howarth

Non-Executive Director 2007 - 2016

Alan Howarth was previously a partner with Ernst & Young. He was also chairman of Gresham Computing Plc, Higham System Services Group Plc and CRF Inc. He held and still holds a non-executive interest in several companies.

D Roberts

Finance Director & Secretary 2013 – 2018

Prior to his appointment at Chamberlin, David Robert had held the position of European Finance Director of Titanium Metals Corporation; he had also been employed by Britax International Plc., Rear Vision Systems.

K O Butler-Wheelhouse

Chairman 2012 – present day

Keith Oliver Butler-Wheelhouse had previously been a CEO of Smiths Industries, Saab Automobile, Sweden and Delta Motor Corporation, South Africa. At the time of his appointment he was also on the board of Atlas Copco AB and J Sainsbury Plc.

K J Nolan

Chief Executive 2013 – 2021
Non-Executive Director 2021 – present day

Kevin John Nolan joined the board in September 2013. Previously he had worked for Doncasters Group Ltd, an international manufacturer of precision components and assemblies, as a Div. Managing Director of Doncasters Turbine Airfoils and Structural Castings Division.

D Nicholas

Senior Independent Director 2016 - 2017

David Nicholas was previously a board director of IMI Plc and held a senior management position at Tyco International Plc. In **Chamberlin Plc.** he served as a chairman of the Remuneration Committee and a member of both the Audit and Nominations Committees.

N J Davies

Finance Director and Secretary 2018 – 2022

Neil Davies joined the board in December 2018. Prior to that, he had held the position of Finance Director at the International Automotive Group, a supplier of components to the global automotive sector, having switched from the same role at Mann+Hummel (UK) Ltd, the German manufacturing group.

D Flowerday

Director 2018 - 2021

Currently, David Flowerday is a Strategy Consultant and Chairman of the Remuneration, Audit and Nominations Committees at Chamberlin. He had held positions of Strategy Director, Group Financial Controller and Flex-tek Managing Director at Smiths Group Plc.

T Brown

Director 2021 – present day

Trevor Edward Brown joined the board of Chamberlin in March 2021. He is also CEO of IQ-AI Limited and CEO of Braveheart Investment Group Plc. Previously he had held positions on the boards of Feedback Plc., Management Resource Solutions plc., Advanced Oncotherapy Plc. and Remote Monitored Systems Plc. et al.

K Price

Chief Executive 2021 – present day

With twenty-five years of experience in the manufacturing sector, Kevin Price joined the board in June 2021; prior to his appointment he had worked for six years as an Operations Director of the group's Foundry and Machining Facility.

A Tomlinson

Finance Director / Secretary 2021 – present day

Alan Tomlinson joined the company in June 2019 as Group's Financial Controller with additional responsibility for Petrel. In 2021, he became a Finance Director on the main board. He has over twenty-five years of experience in senior finance management, including nineteen years in a FTSE 250 construction company.